MORE
THAN
DRUMMING

MORE THAN DRUMMING

Essays on African and
Afro–Latin American
Music and Musicians

EDITED BY
IRENE V. JACKSON

Prepared under the auspices of the Center
for Ethnic Music, Howard University

Contributions in Afro-American and African Studies, Number 80

Greenwood Press
Westport, Connecticut • London, England

Library of Congress Cataloging in Publication Data

Main entry under title:

More than drumming.

(Contributions in Afro-American and African studies,
ISSN 0069-9624 ; no. 80)
    Includes index.
    1. Folk music—Africa—Addresses, essays, lectures.
2. Blacks—Latin America—Music—Addresses, essays,
lectures.   3. Folk music—Latin America—Addresses,
essays, lectures.   I. Jackson, Irene V.   II. Series.
ML3760.M68   1985   781.7'096   84-8956
ISBN 0-313-23093-5 (lib. bdg.)

Library of Congress Catalog Card Number: 84-8956
ISBN: 0-313-23093-5
ISSN: 0069-9624

First published in 1985

Greenwood Press
A division of Congressional Information Service, Inc.
88 Post Road West, Westport, Connecticut 06881

Printed in the United States of America

10 9 8 7 6 5 4 3 2 1

In Memory of
Lula Vere Childers (?-1946)
Founder of the School of Music, Howard University
Warner Lawson (1903-1971)
Dean, College of Fine Arts, Howard University, 1961-1971
Mark Fax (1911-1974)
Professor of Music, Howard University, 1947-1972

Contents

Illustrations

Tables

Preface

This volume, a project of the Center for Ethnic Music at Howard University, is an outgrowth of a symposium on African and Afro-American Music, sponsored by the center in the fall of 1978. The symposium, conceptualized by W. Komla Amoaku (formerly on the staff of the center), brought together eight scholars, three of whom have essays in this volume. The agenda included Fela Sowande, "Traditional African Music"; Pearl Williams-Jones, "Black American Gospel Music in Continuity and Change"; Irene V. Jackson-Brown, "Musical Practices of Blacks in Mainline Denominations: Some Preliminary Explorations"; Portia K. Maultsby, "African Musical Concepts Retained in United States Black Music"; Olly Wilson, "The Association of Movement and Music as a Reflection of a Black Conceptual Process of Music Making"; Mantle Hood, "A New Hybrid? Black-American Vis-a-Vis Afro-American Music"; Bruno Nettl, "The Role of Preservation in Ethnomusicological Theory"; and Doris Evans McGinty, "The Role of Ethnic Music in General Music Education." With the exception of Fela Sowande's paper, several essays have been revised for publication here.

When I assumed the directorship of the Center for Ethnic Music in 1979 there had not yet been established a mechanism for disseminating the papers from this important symposium. It was clear to me—through my participation in the symposium and from numerous requests for copies of the papers—that the proceedings had to be published. I envisioned a publication that would include the work of the original participants, all of whom are music specialists —ethnomusicologists and musicologists—as well as scholars from other disciplines, who had in various ways "interpreted" African and Afro-American music. And so, I set about identifying these scholars and asking them if they would be interested in participating in this project. During this same period, I approached James Sabin, editor of Greenwood Press, with the idea for such a project, and he encouraged me to write a prospectus.

The original prospectus included thirteen essays. But by the time the project reached completion, there were twenty-one essays, illustrating the range of research currently being conducted.

This project has had, it seems, a long history. The first draft of the manuscript was completed in 1981; several revisions followed. In 1983, the manuscript was accepted by Greenwood. Upon review of the manuscript, James Sabin of Greenwood decided that the manuscript should be published as two volumes. The first would focus on Africa, South America, and the Caribbean, and the second volume would center on the United States.

Thus, this volume is one part of a work originally conceived as one study. The two volumes can stand alone, yet together provide the larger picture.

The directorship of the Center for Ethnic Music became vacant in the fall of 1981. As of this writing a new director has not been named. The center continues as a reference and resource place.

Royalties from this work will go to Howard University to promote research and study of Black musics and musicians.

My appreciation extends to all the contributors, who answered countless queries, returned numerous calls, and willingly reviewed many drafts of their essays, and a special colleague who, after the fifth telephone call from me on the same day, answered my question and commented, "You *are* thorough," giving me the push I needed that day.

Many individuals have contributed to this project in both tangible and intangible ways. The former dean of the College of Fine Arts at Howard University, Thomas J. Flagg, provided the necessary funds for the book's publication. Lonye Rasch and Janet Johnson gave technical assistance and were my right and left hands in the preparation of this manuscript.

I wish also to thank Carrie Hackney, former librarian of the College of Fine Arts, for her help, as well as two former graduate students at Howard, Felicia Coleman and Velma Lewis, for their assistance. I hope they profited from being a part of this project. I wish also to acknowledge the support of James Sabin and Margaret Brezicki of Greenwood Press.

To my family both nuclear and extended, who provided me with the emotional support to take on such a task and who somehow endured as a good portion of my emotional energy was consumed seeing this book to fruition, I could not have done this without you.

Irene V. Jackson

MORE
THAN
DRUMMING

IRENE V. JACKSON

Introduction

This volume of essays is about music as cultural expression, or music as an *aspect* of culture. The notion of music as cultural expression was formalized into a scholarly discipline in the 1950s after Jaap Kunst used the term as the title for his 1957 book. Ethnomusicology has its antecedents in comparative musicology and anthropology, with roots in the late nineteenth century. In 1955, with the founding of the Society for Ethnomusicology, ethnomusicology as a scholarly discipline was firmly established in this country. The anthropological component of ethnomusicology owes a great deal to the work of anthropologist Alan P. Merriam, who defined the field of ethnomusicology as the "study of music in culture" in his book *The Anthropology of Music* (1964).

Although there is no one definition of the field and no one scholarly approach, as a group ethnomusicologists are usually interested in understanding music from the standpoint of its sociocultural context—why a music is used as it is, what a culture expresses about itself through its music, and what the music expresses about a culture.

A current trend is underway in ethnomusicology, toward research that is highly focused. Attention has been given to a specific musical tradition within an ethnic or cultural group to offer one example of specialized research. Highly specialized studies emerging in the last decade have advanced research in ethnomusicology by confronting the oversimplifications and overgeneralizations that mar some of the research of the 1950s and 1960s.

Research in the area of African and Afro-American music has benefited from focused and highly specialized studies. Several Africanists can be cited who have offered specialized research.

J. H. Kwabena Nketia has centered his study of African music on the music of West Africa, specifically Ghana and particularly on the music of the Akan. His several books, *The Music of Africa* (1974), *African Gods and Music* (1970), *Ethnomusicology in Ghana* (1971), and *Our Drums and Drummers* (1968), among others, explore African music of a specific geographical area or ethnic group with attention to the sociocultural context from which the music emerged.

Also, Charles Keil's analysis of the function of song among an ethnic group in Nigeria called *Tiv Song* (1979) and John Blacking's study of the Venda, *How Musical Is Man?* (1973), are examples of the current trend—toward highly specialized research. The study of a specific musical instrument within a cultural group is another example of specialized research. In his book *The Soul of Mbira: Music and Tradition of the Shona People of Zimbabwe* (1978), ethnomusicologist Paul Berliner, for example, looks at an instrument found almost throughout Africa but which is highly developed in Zimbabwe.

Each essay in this collection deals with issues about African or African-derived music in its own way. The perspective is *ethnomusicological*, focusing on the *how* and *why* of musical behavior with great attention to the cultural context shaping the musicmaking. Some of these essays look at musical traditions and genres, while others examine the musician as he or she is shaped by cultural traditions.

The essays here have evolved largely from what I call "foundation studies." Among these studies are Rose Brandel's *Music of Central Africa* (1961) and *Studies in African Music* (1959) by A. M. Jones. In the area of African music, the already mentioned work of J. H. Kwabena Nketia must also be recognized as one of the "foundation studies" in West African music. There have been several others who have made their most important contributions in the area of African music through published articles and monographs. An American working in the area of African music, Alan P.

Merriam, published an article in 1959, "Characteristics of African Music," in the *Journal of the International Folk Music Council*. This article, a pivotal one, was to have a far-reaching effect on the course of research on Afro-American music. In 1952, another American scholar, Richard A. Waterman, published "African Influence on Music of the Americas" as part of the proceedings of the twenty-ninth International Congress of Americanists. Waterman's article examined the dispersion of African music to the New World, providing a foundation for the study of African music in New World contexts. His interest in New World Black music stemmed from his 1943 dissertation, "African Patterns in Trinidad Negro Music." Merriam like Waterman was concerned with African survival in the New World, writing a dissertation in 1951 called, "Songs of the Afro-Bahian Cults: An Ethnomusicological Analysis."

The present collection of essays links Black communities in Africa, South America, and the Caribbean. This work has been prompted by several books—collections of essays.

In the field of ethnomusicology, several books have influenced the format of this book: David McAllester's *Readings in Ethnomusicology* (1971), and books of essays on various world musics such as *Eight Urban Musical Cultures* (1978), edited by Bruno Nettl; *Contemporary Music and Music Cultures* (1979), by Charles Hamm; Elizabeth May's 1980 collection, *Musics of Many Cultures: An Introduction*; and *Discourse in Ethnomusicology II: A Tribute to Alan P. Merriam* (1981), a publication of the Ethnomusicology Publications Group, Indiana University.

The scholarly community has not yet been offered a collection of essays that tackles music and musicians of Africa and the African diaspora from an ethnomusicologial standpoint. In spite of increase in publications on African and Afro-American music and in the field of ethnomusicology, at the time of this writing there has not yet been a book, ethnomusicological in perspective, that examines African and African-derived music. Thus, in this regard, this volume and its companion work on Afro-American music and musicians in the United States are singular.

An ethnomusicological perspective allows for the participation of scholars in other disciplines. As McAllester notes in his introduction to *Readings in Ethnomusicology* (1971: xii), there is "a heterogeneity of the backgrounds of the scholars who are making contributions to the field [ethnomusicology]. The presence . . . of linguists, archivists, dance ethnographers, ethnologists, sociologists, psychologists, and others serves abundant notice that this is not a field for the music specialist alone. . . . [There are] almost as many approaches . . . as there are scholars."

This collection brings together scholars in sociology, anthropology, and African studies, in addition to scholars in various music disciplines. By extending the following comments to the whole of Black culture, without regard to geographical boundaries, the raison d'être for a multidisciplinary approach to research in Black culture is expressed well: "Given the complex, multilayered, and polyphonic nature of Caribbean culture, any analysis . . . requires *ab initio* both an interdisciplinary and multidisciplinary approach" (Crahan and Knight 1979: vi).

The approach here is interdisciplinary and the research current. The majority of scholars whose essays appear here have been trained within the last decade; therefore, much of the fieldwork which provides the data for these essays has been carried out within that period. By the same token, the volume also has the perspective of many years of research through the work of Mantle Hood and Bruno Nettl, distinguished senior scholars in the field of ethnomusicology whose research and writing span some twenty-five years.

The essays in this collection are wide-ranging—from the *why* of preserving music to an examination of music-making among several African groups, to tracing a single song-type from West Africa to the New World, to the music of a specific locus.

In chapter 1, Bruno Nettl stresses the need to preserve music and explores the various dimensions of the concept of preservation as it affects the ethnomusicologist.

Mantle Hood argues convincingly in chapter 2 that "while African sociomusical concepts and behavioral patterns have been established as the foundation of Black American music, it is time that Black American music be examined in terms of its own unique identity."

The next seven chapters center on musical culture in West Africa.

In chapter 3, W. Komla Amoaku explores traditional African music and its meaning. Amoaku, a western-trained ethnomusicologist, as well as a performer vested in traditional patterns, relates what *his* music means to him as he searches for the meaning of music among the Ewe of southeastern Ghana.

The Anlo people of southeastern Ghana provides the data base for Nissio Fiagbedzi's discussion of music symbolism in chapter 4. Fiagbedzi looks at the symbolic meaning of particular forms of music within a particular social context.

The main concern of Daphne D. Harrison in chapter 5 is African ritual; she shows how music (and the components that accompany it) reflects certain social, philosophical, and aesthetic values which, in turn, brings the music (and accompanying components) into existence.

In chapter 6, Jacqueline Cogdell DjeDje examines a neglected topic: the musical activities of women. Giving attention to five ethnic groups—the Taureg, Malinke, Wolof, Hausa, and Dagomba —DjeDje draws on ethnomusicology fieldwork undertaken among these groups between 1972 and 1974.

The Igede of Nigeria have hardly been studied at all. In chapter 7, Robert Nicholls, a graduate in African Studies at Howard University, describes various musical associations and dance guilds within Igede society, paying particular attention to funeral ceremonies. Nicholls, whose research was first brought to my attention in my ethnomusicology seminar, regards his essay's inclusion here as an opportunity to show his further appreciation to informants and friends in Igede.

In chapter 8, sociologist Bennetta Jules-Rosette examines performance practice to reveal how singing is a source of social integration in apostolic rituals; her discussion is based on fieldwork carried out in a Central African religious sect known as the Apostolic Church of John Maranke.

The next two chapters (9 and 10) illustrate the African presence in New World societies in South and Central America.

David B. Welch in chapter 9 provides evidence for the continuation, among the *candomblé* of Brazil, of a specific tonal nucleus or scale-type called "melotype," derived from the Yoruba of Nigeria.

The extent of an African musical presence in Panama has not been well documented. Except for the occasional mention of an African source for certain Panamanian dances and drums, little else African has been disclosed in any substantial way. Ronald R. Smith, a folklorist and ethnomusicologist, sheds light on an Afro-

Panamanian group known as "Los Congos" in chapter 10.
These essays are meant to be provocative, offering new insights
and contemporary assessments for continued research and study.

REFERENCES

Crahan, Margaret, and Franklin Knight. 1980. *Africa and the Caribbean: The Legacies of a Link.* Baltimore: Johns Hopkins University Press.
McAllester, David. 1971. *Readings in Ethnomusicology.* Middletown, Conn.: Wesleyan University Press.

1   *BRUNO NETTL*

The Concept of Preservation
in Ethnomusicology

As ethnic music and the idea of musical ethnicity become better
understood rapid culture change endangers the preservation of
musical traditions. The need to preserve musical traditions of all
sorts has become an issue for musicians and scholars alike.

In this chapter, I will examine the concept of preservation as it
affects the ethnomusicologist. Although I will not deal with African
and Afro-American music specifically, my remarks will be food for
thought for those interested in these areas of musical culture.

Over the years, scholars have proposed many definitions for the
term *ethnomusicology*. Perhaps the most cogent discussion of this
term was presented by Alan Merriam (1977: 189-204), and yet none
of the definitions he examined seemed to stress the concept of preservation. Nevertheless, this concept has become closely associated
with the field of ethnomusicology. As ethnomusicological scholars,
we want to preserve the enormously interesting variety of musical
phenomena in the world by recording and transcribing it to paper.
In doing this, we draw on the precepts of anthropology, which is,
in many of its aspects, the study of the history, prehistory, and
ultimate origins of mankind. As scholars in ethnomusicology, we
draw also on musicology, which has substantially devoted itself to
the resurrection, preservation, and performance of musics no
longer truly part of the contemporary culture.

An earlier version of this chapter was read at the World Congress of Jewish
Music, Jerusalem, August 1978.

But to what extent is preservation really an important aspect of ethnomusicology? Let us see first how preservation has actually been carried out, the methods stemming from the many definitions of ethnomusicology.

Anthropologists often define ethnomusicology as "the study of music *in* culture or *as* culture." This definition, articulated most frequently by Merriam (1960: 109), is accompanied by a model of music that emphasizes interaction among three components: concept, behavior, and sound. Merriam (1964) points out repeatedly in his publications and lectures that we have paid a great deal of attention to sound, but not nearly as much to concept and behavior, although these are presumably the immediate determinants of the sound.[1] In preserving the musics of the various cultures of the world, we seem to have concentrated almost exclusively on preserving sound. We try to hold onto musical sounds through recording and transcription. We try to learn something about the genesis of the sounds and musical traditions by examining and comparing the music and artifacts of the various cultures.

Using the musical artifact, ethnomusicologists have tried to reconstruct the prehistory of music. With this approach, we have preserved what we call the music itself—such as scales and phrases —and may even conceivably have come to some agreement about the elements that composed man's early music; however, this approach neglects the concepts and behavior that accompanied and indeed led to the adoption of particular kinds of sound. This narrow perspective need not and should not continue.

Curt Sachs espouses a second definition: Ethnomusicology is the "primitive and oriental branch of music history" (1943: 29). He and others of his persuasion seem most interested in preserving for the sake of scholarship not so much the musical artifacts themselves, but rather the stylistic superstructure, such as scale types, melody types, contours, rhythmic categories, and the like.

A third definition of ethnomusicology that occasionally surfaces includes the study of the contemporary. This definition creates a direct dichotomy between ethnomusicology and historical musicology, which preserves the past. Almost ironically, it is a definition in which preservation can play a major role, for if we are to be students of the contemporary, we must preserve what is happening today and ensure that our work becomes a worthwhile provenience of the historian. In many ways, it is, of course, easier to study the present than the past. Yet in other ways, it is also harder, for one must be selective in choosing what to study from an incredible wealth of source material. One must also select from the plethora of ways to manipulate this source material intellectually.

Although preservation is not really at the heart of prevalent conceptualizations of ethnomusicology, it has nevertheless been the main result of field research—the most characteristic activity of our work. In other words, preserving music has been a central activity, the above definitions notwithstanding. Can we then extract from the history of ethnomusicology some sketch of the history of preservation? Let me make a very brief attempt to trace a few overlapping trends.

The earliest collectors of non-Western music in the nineteenth century probably did not have long-term preservation in mind. These collectors did not, I imagine, worry very much about the fact that music changes rapidly, that much of what they were studying would soon be swallowed up by what they might have called "the pollution of other cultures." They were aware of the effects of colonization, but I think they also believed that the music of non-Western cultures changed very slowly, if at all. They assumed a dichotomy between complete stability and complete abandonment. To them, then, the idea of holding fast to early materials was not a major consideration. Rather, they concentrated on the discovery of what was then a new phenomenon.

Soon, however, a kind of *Denkmaeler* approach surfaced. It began, no doubt, with students of European folk music in the nineteenth century who wanted to preserve the folk heritage. Thus, they developed compendiums of authentic materials. They preserved the most important stories, songs, and melodies of Europe's rural societies and eventually of the Americas, and only later of non-Western peoples. The use to which these collections would be put at some later date, however, was probably not foreseen. They assumed, I suppose, that large-scale, artifact-oriented, multipurpose collections would satisfy a number of future needs—historical, ethnographic, and practical. From such an approach there developed the large collections of German folk songs by Ludwig C. Erk, F. M. Böhme and John Meimer[2]; the large publications of folk songs in North America, sponsored by the Works Progress Administration; the immense collection of Child Ballads by many scholars in Britain and America; the collections of Béla Bartók and Zoltan Kódaly of

Hungary as well as other observers of Eastern European folk music, and many others.

Also in the late nineteenth century came an approach which one might label "applied." Books of music were published for teaching purposes. Records appeared promulgating what might be of interest to the unspecialized student and the amateur. People were urged to focus on music and dance as important cultural activities. Government support was sought to encourage and to enhance musical accomplishments.

The idea was, then, to preserve materials for practical use by the people who had originally produced them, people who were perhaps in danger of losing their heritage. Well, this practice was not without its problems. In the first place, much of this preservation eventually brought with it undesirable political and, in some cases, nationalistic overtones. Preservation meant, no doubt, the intrusion of a collector, field-worker or scholar who tried to persuade people that they should not change their ways, that it was incumbent on them to retain their preindustrial and possibly primitive practices. This intrusion was often resented by people who wished, in fact, to change their way of life and felt that it was necessary to change their music as well. There are many interesting cases of conflict between native people and collectors who wanted to preserve the music of other peoples.

The Australian aboriginals living in the countryside, for example, did not wish their material to be preserved because they claimed that tape recordings invalidate the nonmusical aspects of the material and that recordings play havoc with their conception of what music can do, its power, and religious and ceremonial roles. Thus, for them, preservation of the sound is ipso facto destruction of the cultural context.

Aboriginals living in the Australian cities, on the other hand, felt that they have been deprived of their heritage. They live in a different cultural context, where they are discouraged from practicing their tribal rituals. For them, their country cousins' unwillingness to have their music recorded strengthens the deprivation. What is proper for the ethnomusicologist in this case? It is certainly a question to ponder.

In the 1950s, a movement developed within the field of anthropology, conveniently labeled "urgent anthropology." It recognized modernization's imminent destruction of societies, cultures, and artifacts and emphasized the need to concentrate anthropological resources on their preservation. Quickly, archeologists began to explore, for example, areas that might soon be inaccessible thanks to the building of hydroelectric dams. Social anthropologists addressed themselves to the phenomenon of forced change, where groups of people were coerced to move their homes and homogeneous populations forced to disperse. The anthropologists hurried to study these societies before they disappeared.

From this focus follows the interest in musical styles which are rapidly going out of existence. No doubt, for a long time and until very recently, much of ethnomusicological fieldwork could be placed in this category—propelled by this sense of urgency. We have been thinking that the world of music is changing and have accepted as fact Alan Lomax's model of the cultural graying-out of the world (Lomax 1968: 4-6).

I, personally, am not so pessimistic.

In any case, let us assume we should continue to devote ourselves to preserving our music. How should we go about it?

When we began work in our field, we found ourselves in a position to gather very little material outside Western folk music. We lacked recording machinery, videotapes, opportunities to travel, and so on. What little data we did manage to collect was something to be prized and, therefore, preserved. In the last forty or fifty years, the archives of the world have been filled with vast quantities of music and we are beginning to feel that, perhaps, there is more here than can be used profitably. I certainly have found that the willy-nilly accumulation of archival materials has not led to their substantial use by large numbers of scholars. While tiny collections made before 1910, such as the music of the Vedda of Ceylon, the Bella Coola Indians of North America, and the Kubu of Indonesia, were used by a large number of scholars for important insights, the vast number of songs now extant in some of the large archives of the world seem, by contrast, to be used very little. This is typical for large research libraries. The larger and greater the library, the more likely it is to have a good number of books that are used only very, very rarely. Perhaps this is the situation with our ethnomusicological archives.

Let me suggest, however, that our efforts to preserve music have come to so little in the way of scholarly benefit because researchers do not take into account the eventual uses of the material. Perhaps the answer lies in approaching ethnomusicology as "the *science* of music history." This perspective emphasizes cultural process and change. It calls for the development of field methods that will enable us to gather the kind of data to make conclusions which approximate laws of musical change. It demands that we collect data in systematic, controlled ways so that, as scholars, we can deal with our data scientifically. The data must lend itself to comparative study and include musical concepts and musical behavior along with music itself. We must carefully consider some of the subtle aspects of our field, such as the notion of authenticity (What really is the *true* music of a culture unit?) and of centrality (What musics do individuals in a culture identify themselves most readily? What music is central to and characterizes a society?).

Thus, if we are to make a contribution to the preservation of contemporary music, we must find special techniques to make our preservation significant and to keep our data from becoming an archival junk-heap in which the future historian cannot find his way. One such technique is scientific sampling. In a sense, the history of ethnomusicological field research is the history of sampling. In the past, some researchers assumed music to be in certain significant ways a redundant phenomenon—that is, a single piece of music would tell them all they needed to know about the entire repertory from which it came. Others felt the need to collect everything they could find. In recent times, some of us have come to recognize that merely collecting musical artifacts is not enough, that we must perform more intensive work using sophisticated sampling techniques. So perhaps the history of preservation travels along a continuum, beginning with attempts to make large authentic collections, just for the record, to practical collecting for educational use (in the broad sense), then to the urgent efforts to preserve what would soon disappear, and finally to a realistic, if resigned, way of looking at music as such an enormous quantity of cultural data that only selective samples can be taken and preserved.

In all of this discussion of preservation, I have not yet mentioned notation. In a certain sense, it is not an issue. We preserve music on recordings and it is available for various types of notation. Nevertheless, there are a few aspects that specialists in this area should consider.

One is the lack of a precise and comparative method for notating and preserving the cultural context—the concepts of music and musical behavior. We have not developed the kinds of preserving techniques that modern recording machinery makes possible. To ask an informant what he thinks of a song, where he learned it, and what role it plays in the life of his society is conventional. This we do as a minimum. But it is hardly enough. And yet, we, as ethnomusicologists simply have not developed very much in the way of techniques to preserve other important sides of the musical universe.

Notation is a function of the ethnomusicological instinct to preserve. Before recording was developed and for a long time thereafter, it was common for researchers to derive the notation directly from the performed sound. The kinds of transcriptions from that stage of history are largely culture-specific to us: they emphasize those aspects of the music which are important to students and consumers of European art music. Singing style, ornamentation, use of the voice, and many other parameters of musical sound were hardly observed. This is certainly not something for which we can blame the early scholars in our field. Nevertheless, the notations made mainly before 1900 are neither clearly *descriptive* (telling us just what the music sounded like) nor specifically *prescriptive* (making it possible for someone to render an authentic performance).

Eventually, the distinction between descriptive and prescriptive notation was developed and articulated—perhaps most clearly by Charles Seeger (1958: 184-195). The central idea, of course, is that a description of music requires different notation, perhaps the kind of notation that must be studied in great detail before it is understood. By the same token, someone who is not acquainted with a musical style can do little with a prescriptive notation that is not enormously detailed.

When using notation as a means of preservation, ethnomusicologists have found themselves confronted by a dilemma: choosing between what I have at times called "phonemic" and "phonetic" notations. Both can be descriptive and prescriptive. Phonetic notations show you everything that occurs in the sound. Phonemic notations abstract basic structure in other words, they make use of only those features that are significant to the culture producing the music. The distinction, borrowed from linguistics and old by now, is not without its difficulties. Nevertheless, it has been used with limited success by cultural anthropologists, and musicologists who find this way of articulating sound attractive.

In any case, we must take notation systems into consideration. We can see their significance, for example, in non-Western societies where they are phonemic in a certain sense because they make it possible for the musician to impose distinctions on his style.

Some notations are directly musical. In certain cases, they are associated with verbal expressions and use words themselves as a mnemonic device. Others are tablatures. These systems have been studied for themselves. They have not been viewed as a way to transcribe music in an ethnomusicological context. We have not focused on assessing the role of the notation system as such or on a particular notation system as an index of musical and cultural values.

It seems to me that for the mere preservation of non-Western cultures, notations are now unnecessary. We have recordings; we have videotape. We can preserve rather easily without the use of the printed page. Notation has, therefore, been liberated, as it were, to be a tool for research methods of a more sophisticated sort. Notations made by melographs are incredibly complicated and I think it is noteworthy that they have elicited only a relatively small number of studies. There has been no wholesale adoption of melographic notations in ethnomusicological literature. But it seems to me that those times when melographic materials have been used with success to solve specific problems, these were problems which the scholar could not solve readily by simply listening to the music. It seems, then, that melographic devices are essential helping hands in certain instances, but they are not central to the area of preservation by notation.

The main question we are left with is: How do we decide what is worthy of preservation? Do we preserve what is considered "of high quality"? Or what is typical? Or what the people whose music we study consider ideal? How can we determine what is "good"? Obviously, the ethnomusicologist will have certain personal preferences and there is no point in denying their role. But we must make clear our values. We must decide whether we are going to look for the ideal or whether we want to study the cultural mainstream. We need, thus, to grapple with some fundamental issues of ethnomusicological method before simply turning on the tape recorder. We must deal with questions of authenticity; we must decide what is somehow truly representative of a culture, and we must do this, in part, through comparative study within a repertory and, in part, by listening to our informants. If we are to preserve traditional musics on a large scale, we must face the theoretical issues squarely before going to work. The alternative is to allow ubiquitous technology to take over, to record everything in sight or in sound, and to end up with a type of collection with which one can do very little.

To me, the question of how to go about sampling is the most significant problem of our field. We must learn to design our research scientifically and then to go after the material aggressively. For example, in studying the role of the individual performer, we should work with him intensively, as an individual, and record everything that he knows. To study improvisation, say, of an Arabic *maqam*, we must systematically collect large numbers of performances, and so on. Arbitrary sampling on the assumption that a small sample will always, automatically, give us something representative of a society's music seems to me to be dangerous, despite the fact that it is sometimes successful.

While we may impose field methods on the culture we are studying to gain insight into that culture, we must understand that this imposition may also distort what is really going on. Let me speak from my personal experience.

Some years ago during a project in Iran, I tried to find out how musicians improvised. I decided to use as a sample one mode of Persian music and to try to record as many improvisations as I could. I believe I was reasonably successful. I recorded what was part and parcel of the musical culture. All of the performances I recorded, I believe, would be at least acceptable to the Persian listener and to the informed Persian musician. And yet, I am sure I did not arrive at something truly representative. After all, I requested performances, commissioned them, and thus created formal events of a sort. I no doubt failed to capture certain kinds of musical phenomena that appear only in other, less structured and less formal situations. Thus, my sample was not necessarily representative of the entire cultural universe.

This type of problem is likely to occur very frequently, especially with cultures such as those of the American Black and Middle Eastern or Indian peoples, where improvisation is important. It will surely occur with all cultures in which individual variation from a norm is a major factor in performance. Of course, this includes almost all of what we normally call "folk music." In our zeal to preserve a society's music, we must be careful to recognize the ways in which our preservation distorts the society's musical values.

Shall we continue encouraging the peoples of the world to keep up their old practices? Shall we ask them to do what they, perhaps, do not wish to do, for the sake of preserving the interesting cultural heritages of the world? Shall we make the basic assumption that preservation is, itself, a supreme good which must be encouraged at the expense of all else? Or should we swallow hard, recognize that societies change all the time, and allow previous gems of creation to go by the wayside?

This is an issue that has no easy answer; but, there is no doubt that ethnomusicologists, simply by displaying their interests in certain kinds of musical phenomena, have stimulated the societies they study to keep up, develop, sometimes isolate, and preserve musical phenomena in an artificial fashion. If we allow people to do what they wish (something of an article of faith with me) and then observe what actually happens, will we achieve better scholarship than if we mix observation with participation?

Whatever the answer, I believe we should study change, record it, and preserve it. Change is, after all, a basic phenomenon of human culture. Its prevalence reminds us that we cannot look at culture as a stagnant group of "things." I would suggest that we abandon the musical artifact, the piece, the song, the individual situation as the focus of our study and begin to concentrate on the process of change itself.

This is particularly important in the United States, an enormously heterogeneous country where cultural change is a major fact of life.

As I (Nettl 1964: 226-243) have mentioned elsewhere I believe that of the various components of musical culture, the music itself —the sound—changes least rapidly; behavior changes more quickly, and the concept of music—of what music is and what it does, what power it has, and how it is defined in the various cultures of the world—changes perhaps most rapidly, or at least before the other components. If we are indeed to preserve something about music, we must find ways to preserve and record the conceptions of music and musical behavior. This is in fact more urgent ethnomusicology than the continuing preservation of the musical artifact alone.

NOTES

1. See Alan P. Merriam (1964) chapters 4 through 9 for further discussion about concept, behavior, and sound.

2. Erk, Böhme, and many others investigated German folk songs during the nineteenth century. Two archives maintain collections of German folk songs: the German Folksong archives at Freiburg, and the Institut für Musikforschung at Ratisbon (now Regensburg); see *The New Grove Dictionary of Music and Musicians* V. 7, p. 288; V. 15, p. 674, New York: St. Martin's Press, 1980.

REFERENCES

Lomax, Alan. 1968. *Folk Song Style and Culture*. New Brunswick, N.J.: Transaction Books.

Merriam, Alan P. 1960. "Ethnomusicology: Discussion and Definition of the Field." *Ethnomusicology* 4.

_____, 1964. *The Anthropology of Music*. Evanston, Ill.: Northwestern University Press.

_____. 1977. "Definitions of Comparative Musicology and Ethnomusicology: An Historical-Theoretical Perspective." *Ethnomusicology* 21.

Nettl, Bruno. 1964. *Theory and Method in Ethnomusicology*. New York: The Free Press.

Sachs, Curt. 1943. *The Rise of Music in the Ancient World East and West* New York: W. W. Norton.

Seeger, Charles. 1958. "Prescriptive and Descriptive Music Writing." *Musical Quarterly* 44.

All Musical Cultures Are About Equally Complex

Preamble: Africa has been so clearly established as the source of most Afro-American music that it is time for an additional and different perspective—one that looks at American Black music in terms of its own unique identity.

The title is a borrowed modification of the recent idea that all languages are about equally complex, a notion currently of interest to some linguists. To test this statement as a working hypothesis applied to music, perhaps it is not necessary to substitute the phrase "musical cultures" for the word "languages." Perhaps even the word "music" or "musical" could be omitted.

Under Webster's (1976) second definition of "language" we find the following: "Any means, vocal or other, of expressing or communicating feeling or thought . . . *language* may mean (1) expression that conveys ideas, (2) expression that symbolizes ideas. Bodily expression, whether gesture or (vocal) articulation, and inscription, as printing, writing, et cetera, are its chief forms, but any systematic symbolism, in a more or less transferred sense, is called *language*; as, the *language* of art."

In this transferred sense, therefore, we may speak of the language of music, the language of dance, and, when these two are combined with literature, the language of theater. In fact, the interrelatedness and interdependence of the arts probably justify a phrase like "language of the arts." But if the arts are properly viewed in their total sociocultural context, then we might want to extend Webster's expression of feeling, thought and ideas to include the language of ritual, the language of religious observance, the language of spaces and enclosures (architecture), the language of technology, of animal husbandry, of agricultural methods, and so forth.

This line of extension leads eventualy to a very large hypothesis, namely, that all *cultures* are about equally complex. But this is far too large a subject.

I have chosen, therefore, to use the phrase "musical cultures" to be sure that the focus of attention is music and as a reminder that it is never separable from the culture of which it is a unique and essential part. My testing of this hypothesis has been intermittent and consciously focused during the past two years; however, the notion has been continuously intuited but only semiconsciously weighed for more than two decades before the linguists suggested their thesis. I am in their debt for raising to a conscious level of endeavor something that remained too long a subliminal awareness.

The testing of such a hypothesis requires one more close look at the title: "All Musical Cultures Are About Equally Complex." What is meant by "complex"? And how much latitude is allowable in the qualification *"about equally* complex"?

I have avoided sounding out any linguist in this matter. I am one of those researchers in music who greatly admires and is constantly inspired by the ideas and assumptions of the linguist but one who is also extremely wary of applying linguistic methods qua methods to the study of music. I believe researchers in music should strive to understand the objectives of linguistic inquiry, determine to what extent they may be significant when translated to the language of music, and then turn to the music itself and the culture in which it is embedded in pursuit of a germane methodology.

I am satisfied that the borrowed thesis should be tested. The attempt requires an approach and an attitude, an awareness, not normally associated with the study of music. There are many possible approaches in such an undertaking, but the one I have in mind should foster an attitude necessary to its successful implementation. First, a little background.

In the Western world it is common to hear reference to the art music of the West and to the "high-art" music of Asia. This implies the existence of "non-art" or "low-art" musics and an unspecified difference in the degree of "artness" between the music of Asia and that of the West, the tacit impression being that the latter is patently "higher." Occasionally these references are softened slightly by pointing out that some musics are highly cultivated (in the *Western* sense of the cultivation of music, implying composers, theorists, systems of notation, et cetera) and that others tend to be more ingenuous expression, relying on requirements of text, ritual, function, and the like for their ultimate identity. Prior to World War II, such music was labelled "primitive" in somewhat the sense intended by the art historian's usage of the term. Happily the label was quashed by ethnic sensitivity, but its sometime substitute "tribal" is not particularly apt either.

My personal interest is founded on more than twenty-five years of study and research, first of the music of Indonesia, next that of West Africa, more recently of Hawaiian music, and, for most of my life, of various popular, art, commercial, folk, and hybrid traditions in the United States. I have also been fortunate over the years in being able to place those interests in a truly world perspective, thanks to the research of students under my guidance and to continual contact with international colleagues.

As long ago as 1956, I called attention to the inadequacy of applying such Western terms as *popular, folk, tribal,* and *art* to musics of the non-Western world (Hood 1956: 5-9). I noted that they are even vague when applied to the music of the Western world. In 1959, I suggested using the terms "cultivated" and "ingenuous," when speaking of the music of the non-Western world (Hood 1959: 201-209). Fortunately no one paid much attention to the idea.

Only in the course of the past decade or so, however, have I really begun to appreciate the apparently unlimited number of ways and means by which different cultures may bring their music to a very high degree of cultivation indeed. I mention, for example, the complexity of rhythm and tonal texture achieved in Ashanti, Ga, and Ijaw drumming ensembles; the sophistication of the singing bards (*jali*) of West Africa and the rhythmic intricacy of the *kora* accompanying them; the extraordinary fluency of a master drum like the *iya ilu* of the Yoruba; the rhythmic inventiveness of the *didjeridu* of Australia and the remarkable cultivation of its sonic properties; the interlocking rhythms and tone color of the *amadinda* of Uganda or the Lobi xylophone of Ghana; the recognition and impeccable control of ten or more distinct voice qualities functioning in five different modes and two genres in traditional Hawaiian chant; the very personal but detached vocal quality of a Billie Holiday or the virtuosic flexibility of an Ella Fitzgerald; the eclectic ease of a Flora Purim or an Al Jarreau.[1]

Not one of these examples is ever labeled art music or even "high-art" music; nonetheless each one is highly cultivated, that is, according to Webster: "improved by labor, study or care . . . refined." For the purpose of testing our working hypothesis, therefore, let us say that evidence of cultivation, *by whatever ways and means*, may be considered evidence of complexity. So much for the intended meaning of "complexity" in our title as it applies to this one particular approach.

The examples were chosen to give some kind of random sampling of variety in both the *ways* in which cultivation is achieved and the *means* by which those ways are realized. In the descriptive phrases used in the foregoing text I tried to identify, albeit too briefly and generally, attributes in each of them uniquely developed in the cultivation process. Of course, each example could also be examined by a set of categorical parameters, such as rhythm, melody, harmony, form, texture, and all the other canons in which scholars of Western music place their analytical faith. If our quest were fixed simply on identifying the relative complexity of each of these parameters in our example, such procedures might suffice but the qualifier in our title *"about equally* complex" makes this impossible. How, for example, can we compare the rhythmic density of the *fontonfrom* ensemble of the Ashanti with the artistry of Ella Fitzgerald, even in her exemplary scat singing? How do we compare the *jali* and his *kora* of Sierra Leone with Al Jarreau and his backup group?

By focusing on *both* the ways and the means we can, I believe, manage a reasonable equalizer that makes sense of our qualification "about equally complex." If rhythm and tonal color are the musical attributes that have received primary emphasis in cultivation (and both must be considered together, as a *gestalt*), then the *way* in which cultivation takes form is inseparable from the *means* by which it is realized. Think, for a moment, of the mighty battery of drums and double bells in the Ashanti *fontonfrom*, on the one hand, and the single hollow wooden tube of the aboriginal *didjeridu*

of Australia, on the other. Remember, both these musical traditions have emphasized the cultivation of rhythm and tonal color;
when the *means* of each is considered (a battery of drums, a hollow
tube), the *ways* in which cultivation is expressed would seem to
be about equally complex.

This exposé of our approach is—in the interests of space—necessarily far too brief. For example, in our last comparison we might
also take into account the technology involved. Construction of the
pair of Ashanti *bomma* and *atumpan* demands great skill. They are
even considered objects of art—another dimension of cultivation.
The *didjeridu*, at the other extreme, is a piece of wood hollowed
out by termites. But it, too, is highly decorated, in totemic designs.
Technology, itself, could be considered in terms of its own ways
and means of cultivation. But before we conclude too quickly that
a sophisticated technology necessarily produces a sophisticated
cultivation of music, consider the bamboo flute of southern India
and the incredible virtuosity realized on it. Its Western counterpart
in wood or silver has springs, keys, and pads to cover holes instead
of fingers; it is a technological wonder by comparison. And yet, the
degree of musical cultivation on the Western flute compared to that
on the Indian flute is not "greater" or "higher." In fact, the
mechanics of the Western flute inhibit microtonal flexibility essential
to the style of the Indian flute. The musical cultivation of each is
about equally complex but very, very different.

A truly thorough approach might require us to consider technology, flora and fauna, material culture, trade and industry—
everything that might affect the means by which ways are found to
cultivate certain attributes of music. But, as in our fleeting discussion of technology, we must not lose sight of our objective: complexity in music, not technology.

Understanding, appreciation, even the very perception of the
myriad ways and means of musical cultivation require a particular
awareness and eventually an attitude, if our working hypothesis is
to be fairly tested. In order to highlight this condition on which
success depends I would like to turn to some ideas elucidated so
well by Edward T. Hall (1977). More than most of us, he has man-
aged to articulate some of the problems inherent in cross-cultural
comparison.

Hall (1976: 91-101) identifies high- and low-contexted cultures.
The former he terms indirect and complex, stable in traditions and

institutions, very slow to change, for example, Africa; the latter he labels direct and simple, dynamic, individualistic, and quick to change, for instance, the United States. Within the United States, according to Hall, Black American culture tends to be somewhat more high-contexted than White culture. He (Hall 1976: 14-17) also speaks of monochronic and polychronic cultures: the former being clock watchers, never free of the ineluctable movement of the hands of the clock, driven by guilt when commitments result in overlapping time segments, for example, the United States; the latter easily managing to step into and out of unrelated, differentiated and flexible segments of time, for instance, Africa. He (Hall 1976: 199) calls attention to cultures that "cut the apron strings" and those that do not: individuals in the former managing a greater or lesser separation of identity from the community, for example, the United States; individuals in the latter maintaining and reinforcing parental and ancestral bonds, for instance Africa.

If we use comparative examples from Africa and the United States, therefore, successful testing of our hypothesis requires an awareness of these inherent differences between the two cultures.

Given these and many more individual and cultural differences round the world, Hall speaks of intercultural and interethnic encounters.

Things begin, most frequently, not only with friendship and goodwill on both sides, but there is an intellectual understanding that each party has a different set of beliefs, customs, mores, values, or what-have-you. The trouble begins when people have to start working together . . . frequently . . . neither can make the other's system work . . . without knowing it, they experience the other person as an uncontrollable and unpredictable part of themselves. (Hall 1976: 210-211).

He goes on to point out that "one seldom hears the remark: 'The trouble I have with him is me,' " and finally concludes, "Man must now embark on the difficult journey beyond culture, because the greatest separation feat of all is when one manages to gradually free oneself from the grip of unconscious culture."

The awareness needed for cross-cultural comparison in testing our hypothesis is: (1) recognition of the fact that every individual researcher is to a greater or lesser degree in the grip of his or her own unconscious culture, as Hall puts it, (2) realization that the struggle to separate one's identity from that context requires an understanding that self-awareness and cultural awareness are actually inseparable, and (3) admission that no one ever manages total separation from unconscious culture, whatever the worthy motivation for struggling to do so.

With this awareness it is possible to adopt an attitude that may help ameliorate delimiting cultual boundaries, whether the subject of research belongs to the unconscious culture of the researcher or to some other culture. In 1971, I (Hood 1971: 371-375) wrote at some length about the necessity for what I termed "reciprocity" in the field of cross-cultural scholarship, that is, the absolute need for research conducted independently and/or sometimes together by *both* carriers and non-carriers of the culture in which the subject of research is found. Recently E. T. Hall has stressed the same idea. A proper attitude in testing our hypothesis, therefore, includes a responsibility for reciprocity in cross-cultural scholarship.

I share the interest of my colleagues in wanting to understand quite clearly the relationships between African and Black-American musical cultures. I have tried to show that it is easy to identify particular traditions from each of these cultures that are about equally complex, when compared on the basis of their ways and means of cultivation. But I confess that when I search for examples in Black-American music that furnish concrete illustrations of African ways and means of cultivation—or when I seek examples in a tradition like that of West African Hi-Life, a kind of Amer-African music—I cannot find them. I must also confess that I do not really understand in *musical* terms what is meant by Afro-American music unless it is the kind of quasi-Afro-quasi-Black mixture that occurs as a freewheeling, music-dance jam session, for example, on the quad at Berkeley on a Saturday afternoon.

Let me conclude with the following observations. It is extremely vague if not meaningless to attempt to speak of African musical culture or American musical culture or even Black-American musical culture, because each is so diverse, so variable that only this or that specific tradition furnishes musically significant examples. In the Americas, in Africa, in any segment of the globe the grinding, cutting edges of internal and external forces are continually at work reshaping, refashioning, recreating anew the varied forms of culture expressed through the arts. This was as true in ancient times as it is in a jet-age when Telstar produces instant worldwide communication. For example, historians of music sometimes refer to the Golden Age of Greece, around the sixth and fifth centuries B.C., as the earliest beginnings of Western music. But they are wrong. The foundations of Western music that came together in Greece originated from Mesopotamia beginning around 4000 B.C., from Egypt somewhat later, from the effects of Indus Civilization on both these ancient cultures, and from the peoples residing along the trade routes between Mesopotamia and the Aegean coast. Where were the earliest beginnings of Western music? Well, there is one more possible ingredient: prior to 4000 B.C., Egypt was populated by African tribes, including Semitic immigrations, living under separate local chieftains. Yes, the roots of Western music are richly varied, indeed.

By the same token, the specific ways and means of musical cultivation were brought to the Americas, both North and South, by African slaves. For generations, this cultivation has been subject to the forces of internal and external change. Meanwhile, the African roots from which these musical traditions originated have also been changing for many generations. So that today, in my judgment, Black music in the Americas, both North and South, has achieved its own very distinct forms of complexity, achieved in terms of its own highly varied ways and means of cultivation. Black music in the United States and traditional African music are very *different* in their kinds of cultivation, and in the sociocultural contexts that produced the ways and means by which cultivation has taken place. As implied in our Preamble, it is time to seek a deeper relationship between African and Black-American musical cultures by concentrating on their *differences*. Only then, I believe, shall we truly understand their common bonds.

NOTES

1. The reader is referred to the following recordings: *Africa East and West* (I.E. records, produced by Institute of Ethnomusicology, U.C.L.A., for African Studies Center) Side 1, Sections 2 and 4 and Side 2, Bands 1, 3, 5; Billie Holiday, "Time on My Hands," recorded in 1940 (no details available); Ella Fitzgerald, "One-Note Samba," *Montreux* '77 (Pablo

2308206); Flora Purim, "Everyday Everynight" (Warner K-3168); and Al
Jarreau, "Take Five" *Look to the Rainbow* (Warner 2BZ-3052); field
recordings, traditional Hawaiian chants, "Hele Mai A Kalani," recorded in
1962 (Archive of the Bishop Museum, Honolulu, Hawaii).

REFERENCES

Hall, Edward T. 1976. *Beyond Culture*. Garden City, N.Y.: Doubleday,
      Anchor Press.
Hood, Mantle. 1956. "Folk Imitations of the Javarene Garuelan." *Viltis* 5.
_____. 1959. "The Reliability of Oral Tradition." *Journal American
      Musicological Society* 12.
_____. 1971. *The Ethnomusicologist*. New York: McGraw-Hill.

Toward a Definition of Traditional African Music: A Look at the Ewe of Ghana

In the last decade there has been an increased interest in African music. Amateur as well as professional scholars have invaded Africa in a manner hitherto unknown. As scholarship in African music acquires greater dimensions, scholars are becoming increasingly heuristic in their attempts to challenge a number of complex myths that surround the music of traditional African societies. Results of such studies have been handed to the scholarly community in different forms. The hypothetical and subjective nature of most of the studies has generated more questions than answers.

There have been a number of Western scholars who have written extensively on African music, but many have never visited or resided in Africa for any length of time. There are others who have written "authoritatively" on African music who may have spent a few months or years as missionaries or colonial civil servants in a particular country. It is in this way that the theoretical foundations of African music—which many other writers subsequently followed —were laid by Western scholars. For the most part, there has not been a consistent effort to view African music from a perspective devoid of the shackles of Western thought and philosophy. The most heralded studies of traditional African music by Western-trained Africans rely heavily on Western-formulated or Western-derived theories and methodologies—so much so that these studies are blueprints of Paul Henry Lang's *Music in Western Civilization* (1941) or Donald Grout's *History of Western Music* (1960) and are thus rendered inadequate.

Traditional African music does not lend itself to scrutiny within the confines of Western theories. Traditional African music is not Western music and cannot, therefore, be studied as such. Any attempt to do so will be misleading and only tend to be descriptive, which often is the case.

Since traditional African music is integrally linked with the world view of African societies, any method devised and formulated for its study must preserve the integrity of the life-styles within which the music is cultivated. Merriam (1965: 463) describes the music universe as "infinite." This description is true of traditional African societies in which music, a pervasive symbol, enters practically every aspect of life.

As a traditional performing artist, born and bred in a traditional African setting, surrounded by relatives who are well vested in traditional patterns of everyday life, I would like to express in this essay what my music means to me. But first let us look at what various scholars have given us in the way of a definition of African music. Nketia (1974: 3-4) does not offer a definition as such but divides the African continent into two parts—north and south—and observes that while the musical traditions of the north belong to the Oriental family of modal music and cannot, on stylistic grounds, be included in the family of indigenous African music, those varieties of Western music cultivated in the southern portion of the continent by European settler populations and by Africans of Western orientation must also be excluded from the family of musical styles.

There are writers who have attempted a definition of some sort. Francis Bebey (1969: vi) sees African music as "fundamentally a collective art . . . a communal property whose spiritual qualities are shared and experienced by all." John Miller Chernoff (1979: 28) defines African music as an art form "admired mostly as a spontaneous and emotional creation, an uninhibited, dynamic expression of vitality." Mbiti (1970: 87) defines African music as "that aspect of traditional African life which provides the repositories of traditional beliefs, ideas, wisdom and feelings."

Theoretically, each of the above definitions may be accepted on its own merit; however, it does not necessarily represent the absolute of what music means to the traditional African. Let us pause momentarily to ponder another question: "What is music?"

A prima facie answer, of course, will be, "Music is organized sound." In fact, Webster's *New Collegiate Dictionary* (1973) defines music as "the science or art of ordering tones or sounds in succession, in combination, and in temporal relationships to produce a composition having unity and continuity."

In contrast, Willi Apel (1969: 548) in defining music proposes that we accept Boethius' concept, describing it as "an all-embracing 'harmony of the world,' divided into musica mundana (harmony of the universe), musica humana (harmony of the human soul and body), and musica instrumentalis (music as actual sound)." Boethius' concept applies in a homogeneous society, which is bound by a pervasive world view, where music is an art form that transcends the boundaries of the physical world. This perspective blends with Sowande's view that there are actually three tiers of music—(1) music of the cosmos or the gods, (2) the psychological and symbolical, and (3) mathematical or structural music.

Indisputably, traditional African music is psychologically and symbolically, rather than mathematically and structurally, conceived. It is symbolic because it is a potent, vital source of life, and psychological, because it is intricately bound up with the psyche. It is for these reasons that Sowande (1969: 18) sees fit to define music as

The organization of the raw material of sound into formal and structural patterns that are meaningful and generally acceptable to that society in which the organization has taken place; patterns that relate directly and in a most intimate manner to the World View and the life experiences of that society viewed as a homogeneous whole, and are accepted as such by that society.

This definition is not only relevant to traditional African music but also negates the prevalent nonsense that music is an international language. Furthermore, a definition such as Sowande's reminds us of a distinct difference between societies: traditional societies emphasize the importance of psychic energy and the development of the individual's intuition while those in the West create artificial barriers which interfere with life force or psychic energy, emphasizing instead the individual's intellectual rather than intuitive growth. The artist in such a society emphasizes the entertainment and commercial value of his art form which Hakasson (1967) observes as "thanatism," which implies that art in civilized society is a result of a repressive sublimation of the libido. It produces an aesthetic effect only at a high cost in pain, discontent, and isolation. It is accepted by the majority of the members of the society as a form of entertainment and commercial product. Therefore, repressive sublimation of libido = "civilized" art = inanatos (death instinct). Hakasson (1967), on the contrary, believes that art in primitive societies is a result of non-repressive sublimation of the libido. It produces an aesthetic effect that is both gratifying and vital and is a useful social phenomenon, leading to participation of the artist-craftsman with the fellow members of his community in the use of his work, generally in dancing, rituals, and feasts. It is not an object of trade. Therefore, non-repressive sublimation of libido = "primitive" art = .Eros (life-instinct).

The more potent African music must be viewed within the context of a traditional African life-style, for it is this potent life-style that gives it its meaning and vitality. An Ewe myself, I have chosen the Ewe of Southeastern Ghana as my primary case study.

As I have pursued Western education, I have found that my ethnic affiliations, traditional training, and resultant experiences often conflict with Western perspectives.

As in other traditional African societies, an all-encompassing world view controls the Ewe existence. This view, accepted by all Ewe, holds that the invisible world of spirit, the world of man, and the visible world of nature form an indivisible unit; that the visible world of nature is the reflection of the true, invisible world of spirit. It follows that the "mundane" world is unreal, that man is as much an offspring of the visible world of nature as he is of the invisible world of spirit, that there is but one life that manifests itself at all levels throughout the three worlds. As a result, there is no such thing as "dead" or "lifeless" matter. And because man contains within himself portions both of the world of spirit and of nature, he is, therefore, able to function effectively in either world, but is responsible and accountable to both worlds.

A world view is much more than a mere intellectual concept. It expresses an attitude that reaches down to the very fabric of our being and thereby conditions our psychic and spiritual forces in the most comprehensive manner. In this context, man is essentially spirit, even if encased in flesh for a time.

In a society such as the Ewe, therefore, the classificatory system of music—although valid in the European West—cannot be applied. Western European classical music is an outgrowth of an idea that is expressed in musical notation. Its composer exercises the rights of ownership. In contrast, music among the Ewe is viewed as an expression of a psychological situation, which involves the visible as well as the invisible worlds. It envelops the society as a unit and music makers are not isolated individuals, but inseparable parts of that unitary whole. Indeed, the entire body of traditional art forms is deeply rooted in mythology, legends, and folklore. The archetypal and cosmic importance of these art forms is expressed specifically in those myths directly associated with the gods, ancestors, or heroes. The relationship between art forms and religion is organic, for each is an expression of the same basic fact, which Eliade (1971) describes as "a function of the archetype."

An "archetype," a term coined by Jung, implies prototypic phenomena which form the content of the collective as well as the individual's unconscious and are assumed to reflect universal human thoughts found in all life-styles. A society that derives its life force from archetypes believes that all conscious behavior is a repetition of what has been done before and, therefore, its life becomes a ceaseless repetition of events initiated by others. An event acquires meaning and reality because it repeats a primordial act.

The stability of everyday life among the Ewe, as among other traditional African societies, is dependent on the spiritual vitality of traditional institutions which, in turn, provide solace for its art forms. Traditional African institutions are not mere behaviorial patterns, for they constitute a life-style that has been handed down from generation to generation over a period of many centuries within a homogeneous, closed social unit. The specific origins of a life-style are lost in the midst of antiquity. The life-style is an outgrowth of oral tradition within a society that claims common ancestry and shares a philosophy of the universe.

The Ewe have demonstrated consistently in their ritualization of practically every aspect of traditional music that, indeed, no musical activity is devoid of the Ewe world view. I have never participated in a traditional musical activity in which there was no allusion to the gods or spirits, some gesture intended to link the visible with the invisible world. The degree to which a particular musical activity involves the gods or spirits may be determined by the role that particular musical type plays in the society. Thus, we may distinguish between those activities that are ritually or ceremonially restricted by particular religious requirements and those that, although not directly restricted by these requirements, are indirectly controlled by the community's overall belief systems.

Musical activities that are ritually or ceremonially restricted may fall into the Ritual or Ceremonial classificatory categories. The organization of music in traditional African societies essentially reflects these societies' philosophy of the universe which I referred to earlier as "World View." A ritually restricted musical activity, therefore, is one which occupies the uppermost level of the society. The ritualization of the event is of primary importance; without the ritualization the ensuing musical activity is meaningless. The ritual and musical activity are inseparable. Because of the importance of such activities in the traditional society, there are restrictions which forbid the use of any type of music associated with either a public or a private ritual.

Ceremonial and ritual events are not clearly distinguishable from one another, for the observation of the former involves some degree of ritualization. A ritual performed as part of a funeral of an accidental death is different from that performed on a festive occasion or celebration only in the degree of importance, although both may be restricted.

Because of the historical, spiritual, and social nature of songs, each song carries within it an intrinsic emotional value commensurate with the musical type with which it is identified. Most traditional songs generate or heighten an unexplainable emotional upliftment, irrespective of the occasion on which the songs are performed. There are songs that create instant spiritual tension because of their historical, religious, or social significance. Similarly, there are those songs that may be enjoyed either because they possess artistic beauty or because the texts are reminiscent of an event in the everyday life of an individual or a community.

For example, while most Ewes recognize *Adabatram* as the medium of a god, they regard *Gowu* as the music of the court and not representative of any particular god. Still *Gowu* may generate substantial spiritual upliftment. Similarly, music associated with the events of the life cycle may not be regarded as the medium of particular gods, but may serve spiritual functions.

I recall vividly a number of ritual, ceremonial, and recreational occasions when the singing of particular songs or playing of certain drum patterns drastically altered the mode of performance. I particularly recall those rituals performed in our household in which my aunt, a priestess, would avoid the singing of certain songs if she did not want to be possessed by a god. (Some of these occasions are so sacred to me that I feel uneasy discussing them in this essay!)

My personal observations thus create a justifiable reason to reject any definition of music that is not all-embracing. It is not enough to say that African music is music south of the Sahara or that music is the science or art of ordering tones or sounds in succession. This is not what my music means to me. I can define traditional African music only from within the Ewe world view. For me, it is the involuntary alteration that occurs in my psyche, the spiritual upliftment, my transcendental imaginations of a spirit world, my oneness with the gods and spirits of departed relatives, and that temporary transformation of my physical body into spirit. Whenever I participate in this music, whether physically or silently, I look for the properties that make the activity spiritually satisfying and fulfilling—properties that link me with the invisible world and constantly remind me of a world beyond, in which I believe without asserting it to myself.

To me, traditional African music is the phonic expression of psychic experiences generated within the spiritual framework of traditional institutions which, in turn, constitute the basis of society. These psychic experiences belong to and are revered by all members of the society, a homogeneous unit with common ancestry and a shared world view. Traditional African music is symbolic, an expression and validation of psychic energy. African music is a living thing ensouled by the spiritual energy that travels through it. It is not an object for trade, but a unifying factor in traditional African societies.

I must stress that although I have focused on the spiritual essence of traditional African music, in this essay I do not wish to negate its artistic value.[1] Surely, there is artistic value in every art form. The singer, drummer, and dancer must manifest in their performances those artistic qualities that give the musical type its distinct character. A dancer is considered a good dancer because he or she executes movement sequences that are contextually acceptable within the requirements of the given dance. Similarly, a good singer or drummer is regarded as such because he or she possesses special qualities for the expression of the given art form. But, essentially, artistic expressions are also determined by the world view of the society and not in isolation. This is what promotes their ability to stand the test of time in an oral tradition that is centuries old.

Elsewhere (Amoaku 1975), I stated that it is absolutely imperative for the African and Western European scholar to desist from the temptation to see African music through European eyes, for such an approach will only lead to misconceptions about the primary purpose of music in Africa. The symbolic significance of traditional African music can be found in the texts of songs or names of instruments. The text of a song, for example, may serve multiple functions—social, religious, and political—which are inseparable to the Ewe. At most funerals, for example, one often hears female groups sing dirges, which console the bereaved and admonish evildoers. For example, it is not uncommon to hear a dirge such as,

Ke me va menyo na mi o,
Ke me va menyo na mi o,
Ke me va menyo na mi o,
'Ta ma yi afe le dzinyelawo gbo

Since you resented my presence among you
Since you resented my presence among you
Since you resented my presence among you
I've decided to return home to my forbears.

In this particular text, the singers draw attention to a family squabble or disunity that is well known to members of the community. The text admonishes the family members for the death and expresses what the deceased feels about his death, implying that he is returning home—to the ancestral spirit world, to those who sent him to the visible world.

A number of dances derive their names from the drums with which they are associated, but it is also important to know that a majority of drums are symbolically linked to the history of the given community through their names. Often their names reflect tonal verbalization of the sounds they produce. *Adabatram* is the name of a drum as well as the god it represents. This name also portrays the state of mind that the performance of *Adabatram* creates. "Adaba" = insanity; "tram" = astray. The names of the supporting drums of *Adabatram* similarly connote an abnormal state of mind. Names such as *Kpoe kale tsi* (curiosity leads to death or destruction) and *Kpenyetefe ka* (my buttocks are chopped off) reflect sounds of rhythmic patterns played on these drums; however, they are conceived more as admonitions that there will be repercussions for those who doubt the spiritual potency of the *Adabatram*.

Adabatram is never performed without appropriate rituals which, in the past, included human sacrifice, an act now superseded by the slaughtering of chicken. *Dum, Zagada,* and other musical types associated with gods are "closed" to strangers and they are discouraged from participating. Natives who are not traditionally associated with pre- and post-performance rituals are similarly discouraged from entering the shrine where the drum is kept. I was never able to enter any such shrine until I was thirty years old and considered to have passed the tests of manhood—that is, until I was considered one of the "responsible" men, trustworthy and cognizant of my traditional responsibilities to the gods and society.

It is the religious ritual that sets the spiritual mood and mode of performance. It is believed that the spirit of the god is manifestly present in the drum and every sound it produces and, therefore, directly links the visible and invisible worlds. This is often evidenced with the possession of some participants by various spirits.

Let me conclude by stressing that as a direct outgrowth of my Ewe upbringing, I am unprepared to accept any definition of traditional African music that excludes the psychic experiences that I encounter whenever I perform my music. It is almost impossible to describe these experiences to those who live outside them. They are paralyzing experiences that prove truly meaningful only to those who are identified with the life-style.

It is also from these experiences that I derive the fullest understanding of my music.

NOTE

1. For further discussion see Nketia (1974a: 79-100).

REFERENCES

Amoaku, W. Komla. 1975. "Symbolism in Traditional Institutions and Music of the Ewe of Ghana." Ph.D. dissertation, University of Pittsburgh.

Apel, Willi. 1969. *Harvard Dictionary of Music*. Cambridge: The Belknap Press of Harvard University Press.

Bebey, Francis. 1969. *African Music—A People's Art*. New York: Lawrence Hill and Co.

Chernoff, John Miller. 1979. *African Rhythm and African Sensibility*. Chicago: University of Chicago Press.

Hakasson, Tore. 1967. "Art and Dance, Sex in Primitive." *The Encyclopedia of Sexual Behavior*, ed. Albert Ellis and Albert Abarnabel. New York: Hawthorn Book, Inc.

Mbiti, John S. 1970. *African Religions and Philosophy*. New York: Doubleday and Co., Inc.

Merriam, Alan P. 1965. "Music and Dance." *The African World: A Survey of Social Research*. New York: Frederick A. Praeger.

Nketia, J. H. 1974. *The Music of Africa*. New York: W. W. Norton and Co., Inc.

_____. 1974a. "The Musician in Akan Society." In *The Traditional Artist in African Societies*, ed. W. L. d'Azevedo. Bloomington, Indiana: Indiana University Press.

Sowande, Fela. 1969. *The Role of Music in African Society*. Washington, D.C.: African Studies and Research Program, Howard University.

4

NISSIO FIAGBEDZI

On Signing and Symbolism in Music: The Evidence from among an African People

Of the several theories advanced with the view toward interpreting the phenomenon of music, Langer's (1967) symbolic one is perhaps one of the more recent. Like the formalist and expressionist views before it, it has been questioned by Stevenson (1969) who, in an alternative theory rejects the need to look at music in a symbolic context in order to comprehend the relationship between music and human emotion. I would like to present a point of view that, in certain respects, reconciles these theories. I will examine the bases of Langer's notion of the "virtual" symbol as it applies to music, and Stevenson's objection to her view, and then proceed to show, using evidence from the musical life of the Anlo people of southeastern Ghana, that music can be symbolic in the ordinary sense.

Langer's view of the symbolic character of music is a complex one and demands our serious attention. She follows the lead of Cassirer (1929) who believes music constitutes a symbolization of truth—the truth of pure forms—rather than merely an imitation of nature or representation of emotion. Langer (1967: 40ff) bases her views for the symbolic character and function of the arts including music on what she identifies as fulfilling a primary need in man—the need to symbolize as a condition for all of man's intellection. She holds that the human brain, as a great transformer, continually converts sense-data into symbols; that these symbols are, in turn, our elementary ideas; and that symbol-making gives rise to speech, an observable human function whose main vehicle is language.

Looking at the logical structure of signs and symbols as they function in language provides Langer with a model for analyzing musical symbolism. Thus, Langer (1967) concludes that, unlike language, music is an "unconsummated" symbol, which lacks denotative function. Therefore, music having no fixed conventional reference has import only as an articulate whole. Any significance may be assigned to music as long as it fits the logical image of the music.

Langer (1967) identifies specific structural relationships in the functioning of signs and symbols. In signification, for instance, the relationship is a straightforward one. The sign induces the subject or individual to take direct and immediate account of the object or event it represents. Thus, on hearing a piece of music, a person may identify it as music and, from a previous experience, relate it to a specific musical type. Or he may place the performance within its sociocultural context. He may even attend more closely to the experience itself.

Evidence could easily be adduced to indicate that music functions in the capacity of a sign in society. The Anlo-Ewe of Ghana, for example; are familiar with a traditional tune that is played on a notched flute. They closely associate this series of sounds with a ceremony for twins. Thus, for them, hearing this particular music is quite often a good enough sign that the ceremony is taking place. By the same token, a villager may readily place a particular musical performance when he hears certain stylistic characteristics that are built into the music. He may listen more closely to the performance in which case the musical event will be a sign of itself to the listener.

Further, musical phrases characteristic of given musical types and played by a master drummer often serve, during a performance, to cue either the supportive drummers or the dancers to change rhythm or dance movement. Master drummers typically herald dance drumming sessions by playing long sole passages that serve as a public invitation to club members to assemble for the dance.

We can make two references from these illustrative examples: (1) the subject can take account of the object or event only after he attends to the sign and (2) in all cases, the association of the object with the sign has its basis in psychophysical experience.

In sign function there are usually three elements necessary: subject, sign, and object. In both connotation and denotation which are examples of symbol function, four elements are identifiable: subject, symbol, conception, and object. We note that in Langer's (1967) analysis, a symbol is what it is because it leads us to think of the object which it designates. Within this pattern of symbol function, the term "conception" represents the idea for which a symbol stands—its logical meaning as an instrument of thought. As one's conception of a symbol is the idea connecting the symbol and the object, the term "conception" is indispensable in discussing the function of any symbol, be it connotative or denotative.

Quite rightly, Langer stipulates that words or propositions are symbols. In denotation, a symbol function involving words, she says, the "interpretant" follows the order: subject → symbol → conception → object (1967: 64). Thus, for example, the Anlo-Ewe (subject), thinking of or attending to the word, *halcha* (symbol), conceptualizes and takes into account the particular species of vocal music—namely, the song of derision and satirical comment. (object). The word *halcha* in Ewe connotes a lyric designed to hold up to ridicule some folly or misbehavior or, the act of satirizing through song. At its best, *halcha* employs wit, humor, irony, satire; at its worst, it resorts to plain invective. The collocation *halcha* designates the song-type that is given to satirical criticism. Thinking of the word or symbol draws one's attention not only to a song-type and song as an object but also to the particular conception an individual may have of the object.

Similarly, the Ewe proposition *halcha dugbāhae* literally means that the song of ridicule is a disrupter of the community. As a language event, the sentence describes the speaker's especial conception of *halcha*. That is, the predicate *dugbāhae* articulates the view in which this song-type is held. Instead of this particular one, other predicates such as *afegblēhae* (literally, is a household breaker), or *habaɖae* (literally, is a "bad" song) can be used as substitutes in analogous position in the sentence. Such alternatives will, however, not change the formal structure of the proposition, the descriptive function of the predicate, or the conception of *halcha* which the individual proposition articulates. As a statement of the view in which *halcha* is held, the view is one and inseparable from the proposition though it is variable depending upon the particular view expressed. It describes a "state of affairs" concerning *halcha*. Thus, the individual (subject), attending to the whole proposition (symbol), would in this type of symbol function understand the view (conception) being communicated about the derisive song or song-type (object).

It would seem, however, that there are other possible patterns of thought in using symbols. Three alternative sequences suggest themselves: first, that of subject → object → symbol → conception. For example, the individual (subject), hearing a song (object), identifies it by name, *halcha* (symbol), and understands it for what it is (conception). In this case, the person proceeds from the musical phenomenon rather than from the word naming it. Second, the alternative order: subject → object → concept → symbol (concept). The subject, while listening to a song (object), recalls to mind attitudes (concept) associated with the song-type, which he may simultaneously identify by name (symbol), and to the general significance of which the ideas expressive of the attitudes may contribute. Third, the alternative order: subject → concept → symbol → object. In thinking, say, of satirical forms in general (concept), the subject takes account of *halcha* (symbol) as one such form of musical expression (object). Or, to take a somewhat different case, the subject, in thinking of so-called primitive music, is led to identify the music (object) of certain peoples on planet earth as fitting into the category symbolized by the phrase, "primitive music."

We note that in all four instances of denotation, the term "symbol," stands for the word; the term, "conception" designates the word's significance; and the term "object" indicates the musical type in question. In all but Langer's sequence, however, the term "conception" could conceivably take in more than just the meaning of the word or the specific idea it represents. For, as will be shown, the meaning of music and reactions to it can come from the individual's psychological attitudes toward particular forms of music—attitudes that may be induced by the events associated with the music, by sheer prejudice toward the practitioners of the music because of their socioeconomic status, or prejudice toward the use to which the music is put. For example, there is a song that became popular among the adolescent Anlo-Ewe in the forties. It championed the notion that an Anlo-Ewe should not marry outside his ethnic group. The song's popularity could be traced partly to its topicalness since it was composed as a result of a mixed marriage in that society. In this particular incident, a young woman refused every suitor from among her own people and married an outsider. She died suddenly shortly thereafter. Although it is debatable as to whether the composer, singer, or listener attends more to the tune, the text, the incident which it recalls to mind, its social purpose, or all of them equally, a song's significance to a particular individual is probably influenced by some of these aspects. In any selected combination, these factors certainly expand the meaning of "conception" beyond Langer's definition.

In her main thesis dealing with the relationship between music and emotion, Langer (1967) appears to believe that, as an articulate whole, music is symbolic of human emotion. She writes: "If music has any significance, it is semantic, not symptomatic . . . if it has an emotional content, it 'has' it in the same sense that language 'has' its conceptual content—symbolically" (1967): 218). "Music is 'significant form,' and its significance is that of a symbol . . . feeling, life, motion, and emotion constitute its import" (Langer 1969: 180). If indeed music is symbolic of emotion, it would appear logical to expect emotion to be the "object" in such a relation. But, then, how do we account for the individual's "conception" in this pattern of symbol function? One way is to consider the subject's own perception of total musical significance or the "significant form" of a given piece of music as the conceptual component. In this sense, the individual's perception would constitute the source of musical meaning. The difficulty with this position is, of course, that the individual's conception of musical significance is, essentially, a private one, even if only at the connotative level. For the suggested solution to have wide significance, then, the subject's perception of the articulate, musical whole would have to be communicable.

If, as Langer asserts, music is but an "unconsummated symbol," the phenomenon of music cannot, by definition, afford the subject the benefit of the conceptual element. If, in turn, this element is absent, the resultant pattern ceases to be one of symbolic function. One is then left with the straightforward relationship of music as a sign that brings out emotion in the listener. When we view music in this way, the issue taken up by Stevenson (1969) becomes particularly relevant: Is it necessary in relating music to emotion to view the one as a symbolization of the other? Do we need the notion of symbol to establish the relationship between music and emotion?

Stevenson (1969) believes that we borrow words that describe the ordinary emotions we experience in life and apply them in our aesthetic response to music. This view allows us to recognize the iconic resemblance that Langer postulates without committing ourselves to a theory of symbolism. Still, there is reason to suggest that music can be a symbol in that a given musical type may become the embodiment of an abstractive view of a biographical, historical, psychological, or sociocultural nature. To illustrate, let us take an example from the musical life of the Anlo-Ewe.[1]

In the musical life of the Anlo-Ewe, four main streams of music were identifiable by the early sixties. First are the indigenous musical types, some of which existed before the Europeans arrived on the shores of the Gold Coast (now Ghana) in the fifteenth century. These include ceremonial and ritual musical forms, recreational forms, as well as forms used on state occasions. Before and during the colonial era (1886-1957), these musical types were patronized mostly by the nonliterate folk, since missionaries generally discouraged the educated Anlo-Ewe from making this kind of music.

The second group of musical types are the imported hymns and anthems of the Christian churches, which were taught and sung by members of those churches. Closely identified with them in style are the original dramatic and art forms (in the Western sense) that the literate Anlo-Ewe composed. Third is the category of the local and imported ballroom dance forms, such as the "high life," the quick step, waltz, slow fox-trot, tango, as well as the West Indian forms, such as the calypso. These were patronized mostly, though not exclusively, by the educated members of the society. The musical forms became popular in the late forties, their popularity extending through the fifties. They were popularized through 78-R.P.M. phonograph records and learned by ear and played by the local dance bands, using Western brass and woodwind instruments and a mixture of Western and local percussion. Thus, side by side with the indigenous popular dance forms were the more Western type, danced to mostly by the literate folk at their social gatherings and formal ballroom dances. Finally, in the fifties, other imported idioms, such as jazz, rock, jitterbug, and swing made their appearance, later followed by the twist and soul.

As may be expected, one's connection with the various imported and indigenous forms of music became a readily visible means of social identification. With the establishment of Christianity and the advent of colonial administration, new ways of life and different cultural habits infiltrated the society. The music and dances of the colonial overlords were gradually taken over by the educated Anlo-Ewe in the urban centers as a symbol of social prestige. Clubs sprang up for teaching the dance steps, and the ability to do the slow fox-trot and tango with all their complex variations became a virtual passport to social acceptance and recognition. So much has it become fashionable that, as the North German Mission *Monatsblatt* reported in 1937, a grand ball was held on the Saturday before the Sunday celebration of the Mission's 50th anniversary, and while the older members gathered together for an evening service, the younger folk celebrated at the ball.

The local and imported ballroom music and dances did not, of course, gain the approval of the Christian missionaries. But, even then, the missionaries did not find these forms as socially unacceptable as they did the indigenous music.

With Ghana's struggle for political self-determination and eventual winning of independence in 1957, however, the social image of the indigenous forms underwent a perceptible change. Collectively, these musical forms became one of the symbols of political, social, and cultural freedom. They were taught as extracurricular activities in the schools; the Arts Council of Ghana promoted their performance throughout Ghana, and, at the university level, an Institute of African Studies was established to study African social and cultural forms including music, dance, and drama. In particular, the indigenous forms became vehicles for expressing Ghana's newly found aspirations. Symbolically, they came to signify the concept of independence, of being Ghanaian and African.

In this analysis, I have focused on what particular forms of music may stand for, rather than on what effect they produce. Viewed in terms of the dynamics of symbolic functioning, the process of taking account of music may be expressed in this way: to a given individual (subject), the entity of a particular musical type (object) that is identifiable by name (symbol) represents a demonstrable status (conception) as it did in Ghana in the forties. Or this musical type could represent a sociopolitical cum cultural emancipation as it did following Ghana's independence. Thus, by associating oneself with the music, one partakes of what it stands for. The notions designated, however, are not specific to musical phenomenon.

They are abstractions from sociocultural and political reality; yet, as such, they contribute to the significance of the musical types. They are an integral part of what the musical types mean to the subject.

Since the sociocultural function of music contributes to its significance for the listener, Langer's limitation of her investigation to purely logical relationships between music and symbolic function stands in question. The notion of "virtual"[2] symbolism to which she has been led by her structural analysis of musical and linguistic meaning clearly does not accommodate the examples of musical symbolism described above. These examples show that Langer's concept of the "unconsummated" symbol does not exhaust all the possibilities. While there is nothing wrong with taking a hard, close look at the musical evidence to distill from it relevant theoretical principles, it is important to recognize the pertinent role extra-musical considerations play. We have to consider the ramifications of the symbolic process and realize that what music stands for within a particular social context is very different from what immediate emotional effect the music has. In other words, we must be alert to these two interacting dynamics as we examine the meaning of music.

NOTES

1. The phenomenon is not peculiar to the Anlo-Ewe; similar symbolic behavior has been observed by Merriam (1964: 241-244) in examining the changing image of jazz in the New World.
2. By "virtual" Langer means "unconsummated."

REFERENCES

Cassirer, Ernest. 1923, 1924, 1929. *Die Philosophie de symbolischen Formen*. 300/s. Berlin: Bruno Cassierer.
Langer, Susanne K. 1967. *Philosophy in a New Key*. Cambridge, Mass.: Harvard University Press.
_____. 1969. "The Work of Art As a Symbol." In *Introductory Readings in Aesthetics*, ed. John Hospers. New York: The Free Press.
Merriam, Alan. 1964. *The Anthropology of Music*. Evanston, Ill.: Northwestern University Press.
Stevenson, Charles L. 1969. "Symbolism in the Non-representational Arts." In *Introductory Readings in Aesthetics*, ed. John Hospers. New York: The Free Press.

Aesthetic and Social Aspects of Music in African Ritual Settings

Aesthetics is a term that often arouses controversy in intellectual discourse because discussions tend to overlook certain salient factors. One factor in particular is that the definition of aesthetics depends heavily upon a cultural frame of reference. Thus, a dialogue on the aesthetic merit of a specific object or of a particular group's creative acts will be productive only when cultural considerations are taken into account. Although there are certain universals that the participants may agree upon, these will prove unhelpful if cultural variances are ignored.

A person's culture shapes the notions he has of beauty, of the form and mode of the creative act. His culture molds his values—social, aesthetic, and philosophical—upon which he bases his response to the artistic object. A people's art serves as a system that reinforces and elaborates upon cultural values. When these factors guide a disucssion on aesthetics the integrity of the artistic efforts and products of any group can be protected from narrowness of interpretation and evaluation. In other words, aesthetic judgment should rely on knowledge and acceptance of the cultural reference system from which the art emanates. The specific nature and content of that system is determined also by the cultural perceptions. Thus, in judging the aesthetic value of something within a culture, we must accept the cultural reference system from which it emanates.

In this study, I assume the above position in examinining aesthetic aspects of African ritual. We are, therefore, freed from the polemics of a dialogue on the universal merits of particular objects and can focus on the elements of African aesthetics as they become apparent in ritual activity. I will describe in detail some ritual events that I witnessed during fieldwork in order to ascertain what principles guide the form, content, and mode of artistic output, whether artistic criteria are the basis for these principles, and how and to what extent continuity of artistic values is preserved in the face of change. My goal, then, is not to state what is or is not African art, but to demonstrate art in operation and to illustrate how one art form—music—uses aesthetics to achieve a social/religious objective. Thus, the creative object becomes a definition itself as it reflects the social, philosophical, and aesthetic values that brought it into existence.

AESTHETICS FROM AN AFRICAN PERSPECTIVE

Aloysius Lugira (1973: 52-57) succinctly describes aesthetics as art's representation of beauty. As he says: Aesthetics is the answer to the twofold question, "What is beauty? What is art?" Beauty is multidimensional, that is, it may be physical, intellectual, moral, or literary. It is multilevel in that one may consider the beautiful as merely pretty, as graceful, or as sublime. Art can become beautiful through human endorsement; however, for art to reflect beauty, it must encompass integrity (a sense of totality or wholeness aiming toward perfection); proportion (the unity through which the individual parts come together and are directed toward the same end); and splendor (a clarity that moves one to experience pleasure upon observing it). Thus, Lugira provides a clear definition of aesthetics unhampered by cultural boundaries.

Vivas and Krieger (1953) discuss five aspects of aesthetics: (1) the creative act, that is, the nature of the relationship between the artist and the object; (2) the nature of the art object; (3) aesthetic expression or the spectator's response to the object; (4) aesthetic judgment or the value assigned to the object; and (5) the function of art. These aspects are further elaborations of the twofold question posed by Lugira and can be applied to the study of aesthetics in any culture. These delineations help us in discussing African aesthetics because they acknoweldge the role of artist, spectator, and society in establishing criteria for assessing art. This is particularly helpful when we consider the narrower definition of a Black aesthetic offered by David Dorsey (n.d.: 7-20):

A [black aesthetic] . . . is the syndrome of internal factors governing a black audience's perception and appreciation of a work of art. . . . [It] emphasizes a distinctive combination and relationship of elements. It [black aesthetic] focuses on elements within the work rather than the needs of the audience. . . . The audience is arbiter, not subject . . . aesthetics is the study of means rather than ends.

Thus Dorsey's definition emphasizes that the pleasure derived from a work of art is based upon the internalization of certain cultural factors.

If we approach the study of aesthetics in African settings in the manner implicit in Dorsey's definition, we relieve it of cross-cultural burdens. Nketia's (1979a) summation in a lecture at UCLA more explicitly defines aesthetics as part of a reference system comprised of social, artistic, and philosophical values, which may be studied empirically. In music, the artistic values refer to the orderly arrangement of music or oral poetry. The framework of expectations determines the choice of modes of performance and interpretation. Within that framework are stylistic constraints, as well as models of excellence. The value of art is governed by social values, that is, art is considered good if it satisfies social values (Nketia: 1979a).

Social values may also inspire and guide the *content* of artistic expression. They may determine the source, media of interpretation, as well as the object itself.

For example, fluency in speech is also highly prized by the Ashanti, so musical practices reinforce this value. Nketia (1979b) notes that instruments use a surrogate speech with the same fluency as the court linguist—tone substituting for words. The tonal quality of Akan and some other West African languages makes this transition possible. Horn ensembles use a surrogate speech to recount the deeds, noble characteristics, and moral values expected of a chieftancy, but the most famous and widely used of these speech surrogates are the *atumpan*, the legendary talking drums which speak poetry, acclaim the chief, announce important events, and so forth. No important event is without the *atumpan* (except in certain aspects of a funeral). All members of the group understand and respond to this language. They acquire an understanding of it through the socialization process. (I felt this very strongly while observing the anniversary ritual for a deceased Ewe man in Accra, Ghana, in July 1980. The drums announced the occasion and as libation was poured the drummers recounted the names and worthy deeds of the deceased and their ancestors. After the formalities dedicated to the deceased, the drummers invited the participants to dance. Surely one must know the language to respond appropriately.)

The Yoruba counterpart to the Ashanti *atumpan* is found in the *Iyalu* of the dundun drum (an hour-glass shaped drum) ensemble. In fact, the *Iyalu* drummer is said to have wider freedom of speech through music than he would enjoy in the usual spoken discourse. The typical *Iyalu* drummer is usually a master of rhetoric. Thus, the dundun can be a useful political tool. The drummer can promote group solidarity through *oriki*, praise poetry, and eulogies. The voice of the dundun is heard on most social and religious occasions with very specific principles governing where it is played and by whom (Euba 1974).

Social organization, in turn, determines the organization of artistic efforts, that is, who creates what in what context. For example, among the Ashanti of Ghana, musical activities, musicians, dancers, and musical materials exhibit a structure that mirrors the political hierarchy. Thus, the greater the chief, the greater the number and value of instruments and ensembles he will own or command. Additionally, a special small horn signal played by the *mmentia* (short horn ensemble) identifies each chief. The highest chief, the *asantehene*, has a specific body of literature played for him by the great, beautifully carved ivory horn ensemble, the *Ntahera*. A group of five or seven of these horns greets and praises the *asantehene* in court. The decline of chiefdoms in Ghana has not meant abandonment of these practices; instead, they have been modified to suit the new structure; for example, the *Ntahera* are now used at the opening of parliament. (It is customary to use trumpets in Europe.)[1]

The philosophical values of the culture are also manifest in the artistic forms which operate within a specified symbolic system; for instance, if the leopard skin signifies the chief, representations of the chief will be reflected through the use of this and/or other symbols.

When artistic, social, and philosophical values relate to the materials of music and provide criteria for the selection and use of musical resources as well as a basis of their interpretation, they provide different dimensions of African music. . . . Aesthetics of "the reference system" of artistic, social and philosophical values in music is held and applied or expressed by those who make or listen to music. Hence, as a system it is independent of or external to musical structure, even though its exponents are embodied in the materials and structure of music. (Nketia n.d.b: 3-9)

Nketia makes an important point here: The independence of the aesthetic system from its mode of expression allows aesthetics to operate freely in a variety of spheres. Yet aesthetic values will be operating because, notes Nketia (n.d.b: 5), "they evolved from the practice of and response to creativity."

Where does this lead us in determining what aesthetics are from the African perspective? Nketia (n.d.b) reminds us that the approbation of those in authority and the ideas of a community's leaders comprise only a component of aesthetic guidance. This contrasts with the situation in the West, where we usually defer to so-called authorities in the particular field when judging aesthetic merit. But Africans, Nketia (n.d.b) notes, "learned to appreciate musical tradition through socialization and participation." While, in the West, our aesthetic responses are also a product of our socialization, we rarely participate actively in music from childhood on as Africans do. Recognizing that *participatory* socialization is a critical factor in the development of an aesthetic tradition provides us with an additional basis for examining musical tradition. We are thus left with a model that views aesthetic value judgment as a product of social, artistic, and philosophical notions and the corresponding cultural practices of individual participation in music. In turn, the notions of beauty as outlined by Lugira (1973), in the problems of aesthetics raised by Vivas and Krieger (1953), and the definition of Black aesthetics by Dorsey (n.d.) each helps us to discern the aesthetic aspects in African ritual contexts.

THE RITUAL AS A VEHICLE FOR ARTISTIC EXPRESSION

As Zeusse (1979) argues, most African religions are religions of structure whose goal is the active sanctification of life. In their attempt to integrate into religion the simple things of everyday life, they are far more complex and profound than religions that narrow the spiritual into exceptional experiences. According to Zeusse (1979: 7-9) "the three spheres of man's life are brought together as a whole—the personal egoistic sphere, the social sphere, and the transcendental cosmic sphere." As he explains: "Ritual is the vehicle by which religions of structure achieve this complex act of integration. Transformation of one's perception of an ordinary object or person from a literal, personal, or social mode to a symbolic and transcendental one lies at the heart of all ritual action." If that is the case—and I hold that it is—then the process, content, and mode of that transformation should embody the aesthetic traditions of the group. This idea is consonant with the concept that aesthetics reflects a culture's perceptions, representations, and use of symbolism. If one of the functions of art is to provide for enhancing religious, moral, and political life then the participatory nature of rituals helps it achieve that goal.

In many parts of Africa, ritual involves spirit possession. Anthropological descriptions of these rituals abound. Although the anthropologists did not observe them with the intent of identifying or establishing them as anything other than religious events, it is interesting to note that most accounts refer to the dramatic aspects of ritual. This is not to be construed to mean that the observers viewed the ritual events as dramas, but rather that these events embodied some of the qualities of drama: persona, costume, paraphernalia, acting, and scenery. A most comprehensive collection of studies of spirit possession has been edited by Beattie and Middleton (1969). In this work, there is a surprising agreement about the dramatic aspects of ritual. As Beattie and Middleton (1969: 225) note in their introduction:

Rhythmic music . . . music and movement, sometimes dance, are commonly associated with possession ritual . . . but whether or not they reported that mediums are really dissociated, . . . almost all of our contributors (to this book) stress the dramatic quality of cult behavior. Usually it involves dressing in unfamiliar, often striking and colorful attire, the use of a special language . . . or vocabulary, and the assumption, often with notable histrionic skill, of a pattern of behavior accepted as appropriate to the spirit. . . . It is the act, that is, the drama, that is believed to be therapeutically effective; whether there is actual possession or not is not necessarily the major consideration. . . . Certainly there is no doubt of the dramatic quality of many mediumistic cults in Africa, providing as they do both lively entertainment and a means of catharsis.

In his own study of the Lugbara, Middleton (1969: 225) observed: "Lugbara diviners are putting on a dramatic performance of some skill, and this would seem to be as important [as], if not more . . . than, being 'really' possessed. . . ."

In a case of an Akan (Ghana) cult, Kwaku (1974) postulates that priestly possession is the central act of the ritual and that the *Okomfo* (priest) is the central figure of the drama of worship. Kwaku, too, observed that the specific elements of drama are characteristic of the ritual.

What does drama provide for the spectator? Catharsis, escape, and entertaiment? Perhaps. But the drama also integrates into a whole the perceptions and symbolizations of certain cultural values. Drama binds the artist, object, and spectator into a satisfying relationship, provided that the aesthetic, social, and philosophical values are mutually acceptable. As it restates societal values, the drama also renews bonds of responsibility.

What specifically are the elements of ritual that contribute to the dramatic effect? Kwaku (1974) identifies them as the following: paraphernalia (in this instance ceremonial); makeup for characterizing the gods; setting, a predesignated place which accommodates the act of possession; preassigned roles (those of the gods to be invoked); and order, that is, an agreed upon order of appearance of musicians, dancers, priests, et cetera, as well as which gods will appear.

Other aspects of the ritual may include music, dance, and, in some cases, representational arts. The important point is that during public worship, both the gods *and* the worshippers participate. This drama is an elaboration upon the behavior associated with the gods. In ritual where spirit possession occurs, the behavior of the spirits, or gods, is closely patterned after the qualities for which each is noted. Thus, the expectations of the worshippers can be met when the characteristics of a particular spirit are manifest during the ritual. The spirit medium, that is, the person chosen by the god for possession, in most instances is a priest or initiate close to the priest of the cult. However, on some occasions a spirit may possess an individual to indicate that he or she is to become an initiate. Most descriptions of possession have these characteristics in common—movement in dance-like form which becomes increasingly agitated, erratic, and jerky, sometimes approaching the convulsive; a glazed expression; unusual sounds or archaic language; and sometimes bodily prostration. If the spirit is warlike the movements will incorporate those gestures; if it is an animal, then its form, movements, and sounds will be similar. I must note here that spirit possession is not to be confused with masquerading, although the objectives may be the same. Music and, in turn, dancing are associated with the gods in two ways: as a means of pleasing them and as a means of identifying them. Certain paraphernalia, identified with the gods, denote their personalities, attributes, and actions. The visitation of one or more gods is sought to restore balance and order to the community and thus maintain the welfare of the group. For this reason, it is important not to annoy the gods. Consequently, there are certain prescribed traditions that must be honored. Specific practices differ from society to society, but there is strong similarity in form, content, and process; and in every instance, aesthetic requirements are met.

Among the Kalabari of southeast Nigeria possession occurs in the context of the Festival of Fenibaso at the beginning of the rainy season. Fenibaso is the head of heroes and the patron of headhunting and war. The festival lasts for several days and involves an elaborate drama during which a possessed priest and the group's young men engage in swordplay as part of a war game. The scenario takes place outside the cult house with the *iju* drummers beating urgent rhythms, invoking the spirits through their praise names. The young men strike each others' machetes in rhythm with the drums and watch the priest for signs of possession—trembles, convulsions, and then headlong rushes into the dancing square as he slashes wildly at them. A half-circle is formed around the spirits in preparation for war-play. It is an honor for a youth to receive a rhythmic tap from the spirit as he slashes, sometimes with vertical movements, then horizontal sweeps. The drummers change rhythms at certain intervals to halt the swordplay and cause the spirit to dance. Each rhythm has special steps for the spirit to make. The drummers intensify their playing until the spirit rushes headlong into the cult-house.

This drama is reenacted on three consecutive days with some variations. Finally, on the evening of the fourth day, the priest of Fenibaso and his assistants are invoked during which time special dress and body painting are used. The square is lit and now young boys, with white cloths tied on their heads to simulate war-dress, circle the arena making gutteral noises. Soon, they are joined by the young men who yell "Ye-asukpe!" The drummer invokes the three priests who form a line at the cult-house door. Once possessed, they clash their swords in counter rhythms to the drums. Following the climax of the performance, they retire (Horton 1969: 19-21).

Ritual objectives prescribe specific order and organization. Nevertheless, their aesthetic value should not be ignored. Special formations of the participants enhance the dramatic effect. The rhythms of machetes and drums not only entice the spirit to wage war or to dance but also provide pleasure for the women and children who add counterpoints with taunts and cries. The great attention given to form and style in dancing may be overtly aimed at pleasing the spirit, but it also pleases the community.

The Fenibaso festival and others demonstrate that the structure of *oru* dancing (which is the formal name) is controlled by traditional prescriptions. The vehicle for enforcing those prescriptions seems to be the drums (Horton 1969: 23).

In 1980, I observed the resident *Okomfo* at the Ashanti village in the Ghana National Cultural Center at Kumasi, which revealed a similar concern for procedure, setting, and other dramatic effects. The dancing and possession of the priest seemed, however, more directly influenced by the music. The setting was a circular arrangement with an honored tree and the cult house as the focal point. The *Okomfo* appeared after being announced by the shrine assistant; he wore special attire and white body paint. Amulets hung from his shoulders and his raffia skirt was a vivid red. After sprinkling white powder around the circle, he began to dance slowly to the subdued rhythms of the drums, the tall *fontonfrom* and a pair of *mpintin*. As the intensity of the music increased, the priest's movements became more agitated—with leaps, whirls, and sudden thrusts of the machete. As he danced, the priest balanced the sacred objects on his head, he whirled with a javelin-type pole, and then balanced the machete on his head. At the climax, his eyes took on a glazed stare as his movements became jerkier and more violent. Abruptly, the dancing ended and the priest collapsed to the dusty red earth in a stupor. The attendants then bore the priest's listless body into the shrine house where he sat in a trancelike state.[2]

An Ewe fetish priestess of the Tigari shrine in Abbossey Okai, Accra, followed similar procedures in a celebration of the burial anniversary of her father. Initiates of the fetish priest *Okomfo* Ahia, were seated next to the musicians who, in turn, sat opposite the members of the deceased's family. The initiates wore attire that distinguished them from members of the family wrapped or gowned in the vivid blue prints customary on this occasion. A summoning of the shrine's spirit resulted in one young woman being possessed by that spirit as she danced. She spoke in an archaic tongue as she greeted the fetish priestess and other important guests. Her eyes did not seem to focus as she alternately danced and walked around the circle, interacting with an unseen presence. When fully possessed, she was carried off and dressed in the boxy sleeveless top and square-cut pants, characteristic of the initiates' attire. Her return in this attire indicated the beginning of her training for the Tigari Shrine. As she sat with other initiates strange sounds erupted from her lips—animallike at times, singing at others. The *Okomfo* rushed into the circle and danced with vigorous leaps, drops, and jerks, partially disrobing to the waist. Sometimes she stopped to admonish the musicians—their music or playing was not as it should be. This created an excitement and tension that steadily built while she danced. When she dropped to the floor she was aided to a seat of honor among the other family members. Although this event took place in a compound in the city, the arrangement of the building still bounded the courtyard, forming space which was circular in its seating pattern.[3]

In both of the above examples, we see an affinity for form and pattern of movement in relation to music. Dancing, defined by aesthetic and social principles, functions as the vehicle for achieving the desired religious state—possession. Costume, setting, and objects that create special effects facilitate the ritual goal. The music produced by learned musicians follows time-honored traditions, which govern not only the choice of instruments but also the type of songs and the order of their performance. Care is taken to ensure that the dancers are not harmed, while at the same time the god(s) are attracted and pleased.

As Nketia (1957) asserts, the possession dance aims not only to fulfill the obligations identified with a particular spirit but also to satisfy the aesthetic requirements of the community. Therefore, participants give special attention to integrating the elements of the drama effectively. Drummers, singers, and dancers who regularly perform during the possession ritual are well versed in how to collaborate with spirits. The community of worshippers, in turn, take varying roles, as illustrated by the Kalabari case (Nketia 1957: 4-8). Nketia (1959) points out that the concept of the gods as music-loving is demonstrated by the careful social control of music. Great effort is expended to choose just the right medium and most inviting musical sounds. The building of an adequate repertoire receives very high priority. One result is that the quality of the music itself attracts new members to the cult.

As Nketia (1959) observes, only in the context of public worship of the gods or deified ancestors does possession take place as an organized activity, although it may occur in other situations. The key word is *organized*. In its integration with music and dance, possession is quickly induced and sustained through the use of special music that is closely correlated with specific bodily actions. Nketia describes six general stages in such rituals:

1. Preliminary drumming and preparation; entry of priest and media.

2. Opening of the dance-ring by the Senior Priest, accompanied by attendants.

3. Vigorous phase of dancing by media, but still calm and pleasant.

4. Evidence of possession as media get more ecstatic; shouts and chants from worshippers; impersonation of gods.

5. Medium's possession by the chief god. Drummers redouble efforts, worshippers sing loudly and cheer; chant continues till possessed; medium enters the ring, dances, then withdraws; musicians become silent.

6. Final return of media dressed in colorful robes amidst shouts of joy.

The aesthetic value of music and dance is apparent in other African settings as well. The Ndembu of Zambia have two main types of ritual: life crisis rituals and rituals of affliction. Life crisis rituals are those which are important in the physical or social development of the individual, for example, birth, puberty, or death. Rituals of affliction have derived from the Ndembu's religious belief that misfortune and various forms of illness—especially those associated with women's fertility—are caused by the actions of the spirits of the dead. These spirits, or shades, are deceased relatives of the afflicted. Both types have their own special drum rhythms, theme songs, medicines, and stylized dance behavior expressed in dancing and gestures (Turner 1967).

The rites to Shango among the Nago-Yoruba of Benin utilized a "highly standardized scheme" for inducing spirit possession. Shango is one of the orisha worshipped by the Nago-Yoruba and Fon peoples. The purpose of the orisha and vodun[4] cults is "the periodic reactualization of the ties that bind living people and their ancestors. Possession trances form only a part of the typical festival celebrated for the orisha and vodun. They are the culmination of an elaborate ritual sequence" (Verger 1969: 50-57). The cue here is "culmination of an elaborate ritual sequence," for therein lies the structure and vehicle by which the aim is achieved. The aim may be regarded as bilevel, that is, having first a socioreligious function and second, an aesthetic one. The socioreligious purpose is to worship one of the orisha, for example, Shango, god of thunder. This purpose is achieved when an *elegun* (medium) is mounted (possessed) by the god. The aesthetic aim is met through the careful orchestration of musicians, priests (*eleguns*), and worshippers in a special setting with a predetermined format, content, and paraphernalia. An interesting example is one of the annual offerings to Shango. In one type, several hundred worshippers and dignitaries gather in a forest clearing in front of the temple of Ogun, god of war. Food is brought, some laid in a special spot, the rest shared. Five priests enter the temple as others remain seated in assigned places. Outside the door, rest three *bata* drums and the *agago* or gong. Each time the priests pray, the periodic drumming stops. When the priests return to their places outside, the drum orchestra begins calling the names of the gods. The drumming continues calling forth the gods; if possession occurs priests reappear wearing pointed caps, leaping, and dancing together, and salute the worshippers (Verger 1969).

Another example, the Rite of Onde, was recorded at Pols, Dahomey (now Benin) (Verger 1969). The highly standardized scheme for inducing trance differs mainly in its seven consecutive drum calls which bring progressive changes in the facial expressions of the *olorisha* (priests) as they sit bareheaded waiting for possession to occur. With the seventh call, the *olorisha* leap up shouting, putting on pointed caps, seizing cutlasses—the weapon identified with Ogun. (Similar headdress and weaponry can be seen on the bronze sculptures of Benin which portray the likeness of Ogun or Shango.) The possessed *olorisha* salute the *Kabeyisi*, keeper of the temple, shake left hands with him, and then touch the ground three times with their heels. The role of the drums is a vital one, for it is not a mere mechanical use of overwhelming rhythm that induces trance. Rather each *orisha* or *voudun* has his own rhythm to which the *elegun* or *voudunsi* (medium) has been sensitized during initiation (Verger 1969: 57). This again emphasizes how important the people believe it is to produce music that pleases the gods, and thus the community.

Among the Anlo-Ewe people of Ghana who belong to the Yeve cult, Thunder-God, however, music is performed only to meet a religious need, rather than for pleasure (Fiagbedzi 1966). Since music-making is intimately bound to religious ritual, it must be played near a cult-house. This makes it necessary for the dancers to retreat frequently to the privacy of the cult-house. Worship is expressed through two channels: ritual performances and the dance. Active physical response to the compelling message of the drums creates an overwhelming emotional upsurge, an intense ecstasy: The dance "almost literally compels the god to descend, provokes the display of the adept's magical prowess, and induces possession" (Fiagbedzi 1966: 2). In his study, Fiagbedzi (1966: 7) found that a set of seven principal dance-songs were used in worship: *Nusago* (preludial), *Afovu, Sogbadzi, Savu, Adavu, Agovu,* and *Avlevu.* These dance-songs, accompanied by elaborate costumes, achieve a variety of moods. Following initially pleasurable, competitive, and ecstatic dances, *Avlevu*, the third dance relieves tension and brings the possessed back to a normal state. The worshippers and possessed enjoy the ensuing sexual references and jokes and the mockery that helps to restore the balance (Fiagbedzi 1966).

How does music meet a community's aesthetic standards? Through the use of complex and interesting rhythms, the structural relationship of melody and words (though not necessarily sung) and the conception of music, dance, and drama as a cohesive unit.[5] Also important is the unity among artists and between the artists and the audience which is achieved since all have been socialized to appreciate the same art and technique. Good dancers, for example, expect and respond to rhythmic clapping. They would not respond to haphazard drumming.

Drum-making is considered both a craft and an art. The craft aspect is the capacity of the instrument to produce sound. The art is the symbols carved on the instrument, fertility and power for example, which communicate to the audience. In Eweland, drums made of beer barrels are not acceptable to religious cults which "invent and conserve all that is artistically excellent in Ewe music and drumming" (Cudjoe 1953: 280-292).

Symbolization illustrates a community's values in a variety of ways. In the ritual setting, symbolization provides visible, audible, and tangible evidence of abstract beliefs and values that otherwise cannot be perceived readily (Turner 1967). It is the responsibility of the artisans, musicians, dancers, priests, and worshippers to raise symbolism to a mutually acceptable aesthetic level. When a dancer refuses to dance or a god refuses to "mount" a priest because he does not find the music pleasing, we witness aesthetic response in action. We also witness public sanctioning that reinforces aesthetic traditions.

Real art is distinguished from counterfeit art by its infectiousness according to Tolstoy.

[Only a work of art can] evoke that feeling [quite distinct from all other feelings] of joy and of spiritual union with another [author] and with others. . . . The chief peculiarity of this feeling is that the recipient of a truly artistic impression is so united to the artist that he feels as if the work were his own and not someone else's—as if what it expresses were first what he had long been wishing to express. A real work of art destroys in the consciousness of the recipient the separation between himself and the artist, . . . and all whose minds receive this work of art. (Tolstoy 1969: 483-484)

That total sharing of perspective is the essence of the African aesthetic. The integrity of art in African ritual is protected because socialization prepares all members of a group to serve as arbiters. The splendor of the whole ritual event is a product of careful attention to scale and degree of intensity in music and dance, across time and space. The elements of the drama merge as a powerful unit to attain the central purpose of the rituals—a visit from the god(s).

Everyday life gains "transcendental significance" as the individual's personal, social, and cosmic spheres come together in a harmonious and fruitful manner (Zeusse 1979: 9). With proper attention to aesthetics, the ritual arena becomes a setting for meeting the individual's and the group's socioreligious and aesthetic requirements, to the satisfaction of the individual and the group. The artists receive immediate feedback on the quality of their works and the participant/spectators receive that sense of elevation that "real" art inspires. Order and harmony are restored to the community of worshippers.

Aesthetic and social values are enhanced and reinforced in a public setting with sanction of the total group. Young and old alike witness and reaffirm the acceptance of values through active participation. Thus, the participation of the young in public settings indicates that the community believes in total cultural immersion. The result is the joyous participation by all in the creative, restorative process in African ritual activity. The sense of well-being permeates the group once again, as aesthetics fulfill the community's purpose.

NOTES

1. Kwame Nkrumah began this practice during his regime.

2. Ritual observed in Kumasi, Ghana, by the author on July 18, 1980.

3. Ritual observed at Abbossey Okai, Accra, August 2, 1980. For similar descriptions, see also Manoukian (1950).

4. *Orisha* and *vodun* are categories of subdeities whose mediums are the *elegun*, *orisha*, or *olorisha*, or *vodunsi*.

5. See Cudjoe (1953: 280-292); and Nketia (n.d.a: n.p.).

REFERENCES

Beattie, John, and John Middleton, eds. 1969. *Spirit Mediumship and Society in Africa*. New York: Africana Publishing Corp.

Carter, William. 1971. "The Ntahera Horn Ensemble of the Swaben Court: Ashanti Surrogating Medium." M.A. thesis, University of California at Los Angeles.

Cudjoe, S. D. 1953. "The Techniques of Ewe Drumming and the Importance of Music in Africa." *Phylon* 14 (Sept.)

Dorsey, David. n.d. *Prolegomena for Black Aesthetics*. Nairobi.

Euba, Akin. 1974. "Dundun Music of the Yoruba." Ph.D. dissertation, University of Ghana.

Fiagbedzi, N. S. 1966. "Sogbadzi Songs: A Study of Yeve Music." M. A. thesis, University of Ghana.

Gurr, Andrew, and Pio Zirimu, eds. 1973. *Black Aesthetics: Papers from a Colloquium Held at the University of Nairobi*. Nairobi, Kenya: East African Literature Bureau.

Horton, Robin. 1969. "Types of Spirit Possession in *Kalabari* Religion." In *Spirit Mediumship . . .* , ed. John Beattie and John Middleton. New York: Africana Publishing Corp.

Kwaku, Patience. 1974. "A Dance and Drama of the Gods: A Case Study." M.A. thesis, University of Ghana.

Lugira, Aloysius. 1973. "Black Aesthetics." In *Black Aesthetics: Papers from a Colloquium Held at the University of Nairobi*. ed. Andrew Gurr and Pio Zirimu. Nairobi, Kenya: East African Literature Bureau.

Manoukian, Madekine. 1950. *Akan and Ga-Adangme Peoples in Western Africa. Part I: Ethnographic Survey of Africa*, ed. Daryl Forde. London: International African Institute.

Middleton, John. 1969. "Spirit Possession Among the Lugbara." In *Spirit Mediumship and Society in Africa*, ed. John Beattie and John Middleton. New York: Africana Publishing Corp.

Nketia, J. H. Kwabena. n.d.a. "Music in Traditional African Worship in Christian Worship." Unpublished manuscript. Legon: University of Ghana, n.p.

———. n.d.b. "Tradition and Innovation in African Music." *Jamaica Journal*.

———. 1957. "Possession Dances in African Societies." *International Folk Music Journal* Vol. IX.

———. 1959. *African Gods and Music*. Universitas, Vol. IV, 1.

———. 1979a. Lecture, African Humanities Institute, UCLA, April, 1979.

———. 1979b. Lecture, African Humanities Institute, UCLA, May, 1979.

Tolstoy, Leo. 1953. "The Religious Function of Art." In *The Problems of Aesthetics*, ed. Eliseo Vivas and Murray Krieger. New York: Rinehart and Co.

Turner, Victor. 1967. *The Forest of Symbols: Aspects of Ndembu Ritual*. Ithaca, N.Y. Cornell University Press.

Verger, Pierre. 1969. "Trance and Convention in Nago-Yoruba" in *Spirit Mediumship and Society in Africa*, ed. John Beattie and John Middleton. New York: Africana Publishing Corp.

Vivas, Eliseo, and Murray Krieger, eds. 1953. *The Problems of Aesthetics*. New York: Rinehart and Co.

Zeusse, Evan. 1979. *Ritual Cosmos: The Sanctification of Life in African Religions*. Athens, Ohio: Ohio University Press.

Women and Music in Sudanic Africa

Scholarly studies concerning the role of women in traditional African music are rare. Very few full-length studies have been devoted exclusively to the music of women. Broad generalized works, such as Nketia (1974) and Bebey (1975) sometimes include a brief mention of music types performed by women, and there are a few articles concerning the role of women in music of specific societies or countries. In most instances, researchers either recount the details about female initiation and puberty rites or make note of certain instruments, dances, and song types exclusively performed by women. To my knowledge, however, no comprehensive document investigating the music-making of women on a regional and cross-cultural basis has yet been created. In fact, an examination of the literature on African music reveals that very little research focuses on the music of either men or women.

This chapter has a threefold purpose: to examine the role of women in relation to music, to give the reader knowledge of a music area that is normally ignored in the literature of African music, and to provide a comparative analysis of the music of five different ethnic groups in the Sudan in order to achieve a broad perspective on the type of music women produce.

Because of the unavailability of sources concerning women and music, the information presented here has been taken primarily from historical and anthropological studies. I obtained material pertaining to music from the notes of recordings and ethnomusicological literature. The primary source material comes from my travels through the Central and Western Sudan (northern Nigeria, Niger, northern Benin, Burkina Faso [formerly known as Upper Volta], and northern Ghana and the Ivory Coast) between 1972 and 1974.[1]

HISTORICAL AND CULTURAL BACKGROUND

The Sudanic or savannah belt[2] of Africa constitutes a unique cultural enclave, which is not often examined by scholars in African music. The Sudanic area covers roughly the territory from 10° North Latitude to 17° North Latitude, extending across the African continent from Senegal to Ethiopia. The term Sudan should not be confused with the country located in northeast Africa or the area called West Africa. While West Africa encompasses parts of the savannah belt, it actually refers to the land stretching from Senegal to Lake Chad.[3]

In this study, only the Western and Central Sudan areas will be considered at length,[4] since it is here that the five ethnic groups I chose to examine—the Tuareg, Malinke, Wolof, Hausa, and Dagomba—are located.

These five ethnic groups, however, do not reside in five distinct countries; rather, they are scattered without regard for modern political boundaries. For example, although the Wolof seem to be permanently settled in one central area of Senegal and the Dagomba in northern Ghana, others are dispersed over several countries. The Malinke are loosely scattered throughout the western Sudan, living primarily in Senegal, the Gambia, in parts of Guinea and Guinea Bissau, the southern tip of Mauritania, most of Mali, the northern Ivory Coast, and other areas. The Hausa are most prominently found in northern Nigeria and Niger, while the Tuareg are scattered throughout Niger, Mali, Algeria, the northern tip of Burkina Faso, and the southwestern edge of Libya.

In order to understand more clearly the role of women in each of these societies, it is necessary to examine the culture as a whole and make special note of the activities women perform. Historically, each of the ethnic groups has had intercultural contacts through trade with Islam, and they also share a number of social institutions. Therefore, it might be useful to analyze the historical and cultural backgrounds chronologically, examining those people who are believed to have first initiated contacts which subsequently gave rise to interactions with other groups.

History

The Tuareg people, probably the first and only ethnic group in this study to have direct physical contact with the Arabs, grew out of the larger Berber group, which had resided in North Africa. The Tuareg converted to Islam as a result first of Arab conquests in the seventh century A.D. and then Bedouin immigrations into North Africa during the eleventh century A.D. Once Arab conquests and Bedouin invasions displaced many Berber groups, the latter sought refuge in the oases of the Sahara; there they adopted a nomadic and predatory mode of life, modeled on that of their invaders. Even though they have retained the language and many of the customs of their Berber ancestors, the Tuareg have developed a unique culture of their own—a genuine synthesis of many traditions including not only Berber and Arab but also elements from indigenous Negro peoples who reside in the lower Sahara (Murdock 1959: 406).

The Malinke, during the eleventh century A.D., founded the Mali Empire on the Niger River. It is believed that the Malinke were first introduced to Islam by the Tukulor[5] through trade. While Malinke merchants and royal elite came in contact with Islam as early as the eleventh century A.D., the religion was never wholeheartedly accepted by the masses until the fourteenth to sixteenth centuries.

The Malinke empire expanded rapidly in the thirteenth century when it defeated the Soso in 1235 and, in 1240, occupied remnants of the Soninke Ghana Empire. By 1325, it dominated all of West Africa. Gradually, however, the Mali Empire fell into a decline, losing power in the late fifteenth century (Murdock 1959: 73).

At one time, the Wolof resided farther north in coastal Mauritania. Due to Berber migrations in the eleventh century A.D., the Wolof also moved southward and settled near the mouth of the Senegal River. Eventually, they ruled a kingdom of some magnitude until around 1520. It is believed that, like the Malinke, the Wolof were first introduced to Islam by the Tukulor in the eleventh century.

Some scholars claim that "historically and physically the Hausa are not a race at all," that the term Hausa "is primarily linguistic, and also to a considerable extent religious and cultural" (Meek 1921: 27). Whether this is true is questionable. Murdock (1959: 137) states that some Hausa-speaking people once occupied the central position of the Sahara but moved south when they were driven out by Berbers under Arab pressure. In any case, it was not until the nineteenth century A.D. when the Fulani conquered them that the Hausa became politically unified. Still, because of long experience in the trans-Saharan caravan trade, they "achieved a degree of cultural unity comparable to that of the great nations of Europe in modern times and are perhaps the only nation of Negro Africa where this can definitely be said to have happened prior to European colonial occupation" (Murdock 1959: 137).

A controversy exists concerning who first introduced the Arabic religion to the Hausa. Although Trimingham (1962: 47) suggests that the Tukulor are directly responsible for their conversion, it is more likely that the change occurred indirectly through the Malinke. Murdock (1959: 139) believes that the Hausa peoples received their first knowledge of Islam from the West in the fourteenth century when the Malinke kingdom of Mali, then at its apogee, dispatched merchants and emissaries to Hausaland.

It is believed that the Dagomba have been settled for a fairly long time in their present habitation in northern Ghana. In spite of contacts with Mali and Hausaland, they have not created great empires or states comparable to those of their western and eastern neighbors. Moreover, the Dagomba have not been subjected to foreign domination to the extent that the Tuareg, Malinke, Wolof, or Hausa have. Many feel that the culture of the Dagomba "probably reflects fairly closely what that of the Mande [Malinke] must have been prior to their embarkation on a career of empire building and to the advent of the Berbers and Arabs from the north" (Murdock 1959: 78).

Less subjection to foreign domination in Dagbon accounts for the lack of Islamic penetration into northern Ghana. The impact of Mohammedanism on the Dagomba—which did not occur until the late seventeenth/early eighteenth centuries—has been slight in comparison to that of other Sudanic groups, and most Dagomba are considered to be "nominal" Muslims. To one degree or another, however, all groups have embraced Islam.

In addition to accepting Islam, several groups—most notably the

Tuareg, Hausa, and Dagomba—participate in spirit-possession cults, known as *bori* in Hausaland. These cults are especially attractive to women. The reason for this, according to one author, is that oftentimes women "are excluded from full participation in the public rituals of orthodox Islam" (Lewis 1966: 64). A very good example of the degree of religious discrimination that occurs within some societies is found among the Mossi, kinsmen of the Dagomba who live in Burkina Faso. Mossi women are segregated behind the men at the open-air prayers during festivals and are not permitted within the mosques because Muslims feel that the presence of women at prayers distracts the men from their devotion to God.[6]

Women also are attracted to possession cults because of their entertainment value and the need to seek relief from afflictions which the orthodox rituals and prophylactics of Islam have failed to remedy.

Economy

With the exception of the Tuareg who are camel nomads, all groups subsist primarily through agriculture. Men normally do the bulk of the agricultural work, clearing the land and taking charge of cash crops. Women are responsible for the cultivation of garden crops and sometimes render assistance in the large fields.

Again, with the exception of the Tuareg, animal husbandry holds a significant, though subsidiary, place in the economy of all groups. They have adopted some of the domesticated animals from North Africa, such as cattle, goats, and sheep. Cattle herding is always performed by men; women normally do the milking, though among the Malinke and Dagomba neither sex does any milking since cattle are essentially symbols of prestige and wealth. Only Wolof women tend goats and sheep; other groups leave this type of work to the men.

Thus, ethnographic evidence reveals that where Islam is firmly established, agricultural fieldwork and animal husbandry, once shared nearly equally by men and women, tend to become primarily masculine concerns (Murdock 1959: 142). The only sector of the economy where women have full control or at least a semimonopoly is in the gathering of food—for example, in small-scale fishing among the Tuareg and Wolof; market-trading among the

Malinke, Hausa, and Dagomba; and caring for poultry among the Malinke and Wolof. Men dominate in large-scale fishing, hunting, and, most importantly, foreign trade, which plays an essential role in the economies of all the groups.

Social Organization

Just as we saw that Arab influence greatly affects religious and economic practices of Sudanic Africa, the same is apparent in social organization. The degree to which Arab culture has been influential determines the particular group's social system. This is evident if we look at the castes that each group has incorporated.

Probably the Tuareg have the most rigid and complex social structure. As Murdock (1959: 118) explains: "The minimal development of social stratification among the less acculturated Berbers contrasts sharply with the situation in those groups who have been politically subjugated by the Arabs and among those who have themselves subjugated indigenous Negro peoples."

The Tuareg have adopted the Arab caste system in its fullest range. In addition to the religious nobles, there are five separate castes: (1) the ruling Tuareg, who lead a parasitic life of warfare and political domination; (2) the vassal Tuareg, who engage in herding, bear arms in support of their rulers, and render regular tribute to them; (3) Negro serfs who cultivate the land and pay tribute to particular groups of rulers or vassals; (4) privately owned Negro slaves, obtained from the Sudan through purchase or capture, who are employed in domestic service and other menial labor; and (5) outcaste groups of Negro artisans, especially smiths and leather workers. A woman is allowed to marry a man of her own or a higher caste, whereas a man may marry a woman of his own or a lower caste. Social status is thus transmitted through women. Caste rules protect dominant rulers and vassals from any infusion of Negro blood and many believe the rule was instituted for this very purpose (Murdock 1959: 407).

The Malinke and Wolof have similar, though less rigid, social structures. It is believed that long exposure to Arab influence accounts for the prevalence of the "despised endogamous castes" among the Malinke, "including smiths, leatherworkers, sometimes other artisans and fishermen, and usually the so-called *griots*, who are musicians, bards, and genealogists" (Murdock 1959: 76). Among the Wolof, as a result of Islamic influence, as many as ten different stratified statuses are found (see Murdock 1959: 268).

In Hausa society, "the major classes are (1) a privileged nobility, often headed by a royal lineage; (2) free commoners, frequently divided into wealthy merchants, artisans, and peasant farmers, and (3) slaves, including debt slaves. In addition, endogamous depressed castes of smiths, leatherworkers, hunters, and griots are commonly differentiated in the westernmost provinces" (Murdock 1959: 144). Among the Dagomba, there are distinctions between the hereditary noble class (invaders who came from northeast Africa more than 400 years ago), commoners (original inhabitants of the land), and muslims (descendants of the Malinke and Hausa missionaries and traders). There are also exogamous groups of musicians, butchers, leather workers, and other artisans in Dagbon.

All groups, with the exception of the Tuareg, are generally polygynous and practice patrilineal descent, inheritance, and succession. In spite of Arab influence, most Tuareg prefer monogamy and practice matrilineal inheritance. This sharply contrasts with other Berber groups who observe patrilineal succession. Murdock (1959: 407-408) suggests that "they may well have instituted matrilineal affiliation for intercaste marriages in order to preserve their purity of race."

Status and Role of Women

Throughout this discussion, it has been evident that the historical and cultural development of the Tuareg contrasts sharply with that of the other Sudanic peoples. In regard to the position of women, they again differ. The Tuareg give their women a very high social status. While the men spend the majority of their time herding, raiding, and protecting caravan clients, household chores are done by Negro serfs and slaves. Women, especially those of the upper two caste levels, relieved of most economic and household responsibilities, devote themselves to the fine arts. Music and poetry are primarily feminine accomplishments; men usually assist, but do not hold any of the important positions in musical activities. While only a few men are literate, all Tuareg women are able to read and write in the peculiar Tuareg script. Further, as among the northern tribes, women own the bulk of all livestock. Symbolically, only among the Tuareg do men rather than women wear veils (Murdock 1959: 407).

In the other groups, the status of women is much lower. Although women's work may not be as physically trying as that of men in Malinke, Wolof, Hausa, and Dagomba societies, women's work requires at least as many hours, if not more. Not only do women cultivate some crops or participate in market trade, but many take full responsibility for all household chores and child care. It is extremely rare to find a Sudanic woman who is able to read and write; only men are normally allowed to acquire training in these aspects of life. The ownership of property is hardly, if ever, left to women. Moreover, women among the Malinke, Wolof, Hausa, and Dagomba do not have primary responsibility for music-making or other fine arts; they simply accompany, or assist their husbands in these endeavors.

Arab influence has, indeed, left its mark on these five ethnic groups. But, as the data show, the acculturation process can be selective. A society accepts only as much of a foreign culture as it chooses to; consequently, we find differences among the various groups—particularly the Tuareg.

ASPECTS OF MUSICAL PERFORMANCE

Function

Practically all aspects of traditional life in Sudanic Africa involve music produced by women. For example, music has its political functions; hence, there are songs in praise of heads of state or other officialdom and songs to rally the community to support politicians; there are historical and legendary songs that record important past events in the society; and there are war songs.

Among the Tuareg, where women have a greater responsibility for the perpetuation and production of music, praise songs form an important part of the repertoire. Praise songs are most often sung to acclaim the feats of Tuareg men.

Among the Malinke, women who are permanently attached to the royal family are the major vocalists at the courts of Mali kings. While men play the instrumental accompaniment, women sing praise, historical, and legendary songs, glorifying important personages in Malinke history.

Occasionally, Wolof female slaves (known as *jam i gewel*) sing praises in honor of royalty at the king's palace for events of the life cycle such as birth ceremonies. They provide their own instrumental accompaniment by clapping hands and playing gourd drums.

In Hausaland, there is a female professional praise singer for the *Emir* (ruler), known as *zabiyai Sarki*. She is permanently attached to the royal court and sings for the *Emir* at the weekly homage and feast of his wives and for all royal cavalcades. In addition, she performs every day as she escorts the *Emir* from the wives' quarters of the palace to the Council Chamber and back again (Ames and King 1971: 94).

Women in Dagbon serve only as assistants to men who perform during political occasions. Most famous are the young women who sing choral responses and play rattles with one-string fiddle performers at the royal feasts, weekly homage, and other royal occasions. There are also female praise singers who accompany drummers during certain religious feasts at the royal palace (Kinney 1970: 263-264). In all instances, Dagomba women never perform at any of these activities in the presence of the king while he is alone, nor without the accompaniment of male musicians, as is the case in Hausaland. Genealogical, praise, and war songs constitute the repertoire at these events.

It is during life cycle events and other social activities that women participate more actively in music-making. During birth rituals and weddings, in many cases, women are the only participants. Frequently, women sing lullabies, courting songs, and also educational songs to teach their older children. Although no documented evidence is available, it is probable that women also take part in rites of passage for young girls if and when they occur in the culture. In observing the Dagomba, I noted that women normally assist men at funeral celebrations in performing songs in honor and praise of the deceased and his family.

Songs that comment on a particular aspect of family or community life are also performed by women in Sudanic Africa. Professional female singers, sometimes hired to entertain women at marriage feasts, may, for example, sing critical songs. "Songs ridi-

culing co-wives are especially popular" (Ames and King 1971: 91).·
Songs are also performed for economic reasons. Not only does
the music make the work a lot less monotonous, but it is believed to
increase the efficiency of the cooperative labor. Women all over
Africa are known to create music while doing household chores,
such as cooking and cleaning, and those in the Sudan are no exception. For example, women sing daily as they grind corn or pound
pestles in a mortar.

The hunting music performed by a Malinke woman or the songs
sung by Tuareg females at a camel-herding event are different in
character from these work songs in that they are not performed
while working and do not arise from the work experience. Rather,
they are similar to praise songs because through them the women
congratulate the men for their labor and encourage them to continue.

In Sudanic Africa, two types of religious songs are performed:
one for Islamic rituals and the other for ceremonies of the possession cult. Men are generally the leading performers at Islamic
events, while women, such as those in Malinke and Dagomba
cultures, usually accompany and assist them. During cult activities,
the opposite is the case; women play a major role in music-making
during *bori* celebrations. In Tuareg society, women use possession
music to help cure mental and physical disorders. They alone sing,
dance, and play drum accompaniment. The performance of *bori*
music is especially popular with harlots in Hausaland. The performance of this music is often used for entertainment purposes at
festivals or wedding ceremonies, but like the Tuareg, it is also used
for healing the mentally and physically ill. In spite of its nonaccep-
tance by pious Muslims, *bori* music is extremely popular and *bori*
musicians have become wealthy in comparison to other occupational groups in the society.

Music for entertainment purposes includes songs of all types—
for example, love, humorous, praise, political, and historical.
During festive occasions, such as the celebration of Muslim holidays, women sometimes accompany men in playing music, both
for royalty and for commoners. At these occasions, the popular
historical and praise songs can be heard. Some are performed during public parades or political rallies. Other performances are given
for women in the privacy of homes when they come together to
celebrate festivals while in *purdah* (seclusion). In addition, prosti-

tutes often entertain patrons and clients in harlot houses by singing popular songs of the day. It is noteworthy that in Mali, women sing love songs while men play instrumental accompaniment. Among the Tuareg, it is the men who do the singing, while women play the instruments. Women often perform music as men dance. They sing and provide rhythmic accompaniment by clapping their hands and tapping their feet. Among the Tuareg, there is a song type known as *ezelé*, which specifically refers to compositions performed by women to accompany male dancing.

Instruments

Instruments from the four classification groups—idiophones, membranophones, chordophones, and aerophones—are played by women of Sudanic Africa. Some play a wide variety of instrumental types, while others are proficient in only one or two. This fact is important, for it gives an indication of the role that women play in producing music in a particular society. For example, Tuareg women play all the major instruments except the flute and they are almost solely responsible for the continuity of musical traditions in Tuareg society. The flute (*sareoua* or *tassansirkh* is played by male shepherds who belong to the servant caste, but women play the *imzad* (*amz'ah*), a one-string fiddle; the single-headed drum known as *tinde*; and gourd water drum.

The term *imzad* (plural, *imzaden*) means hair and the bowstring used for this instrument is made from the hair of women (Holiday 1956: 50). With the fiddle, women most often accompany love songs sung by men. Because of the fiddle's delicate tone and lack of volume, some scholars believe the fiddle is symbolic of the female voice in a performance situation, "the necessary complement to a declaration of love" (Holiday 1956: 50-51).

The *tinde* primarily accompanies songs of praise (*tinde nomnas*) and possession (*tinde n'gouma*)—songs which are all performed by women (Nikiprowetzky 1966: 55). Although drum rhythms that accompany these songs contain fewer intricate cross rhythms than those performed by Tuareg sedentary neighbors in the south, the chantlike quality of the women's singing suggests Negro influence (Holiday 1956: 50-51).

The gourd and bowl of water used in the construction of the gourd water drum suggest that this instrument "is a recent innovation, since bowls are not readily obtainable in the Sahara except through foreign manufacture and trade, that is, foreign to the Tuareg" (Holiday 1956: 50). With the water drum, women provide accompaniment for dance and wedding music as well as camel songs.

Among the Malinke, documentation reveals only two types of idiophones—metal scrapers and gourd rattles—being played by women. The idiophones primarily accompany string, xylophone, and drum music at festive and dance occasions; however, unlike the Tuareg, the Malinke reserve none of these instruments exclusively for females.

Even fewer instrumental types have been documented for the Wolof and Dagomba. Wolof women sometimes use an overturned gourd bowl, placed on a pillow, as percussive accompaniment to praise singing. It is either beaten with bare hands or struck with a stick. In both societies, only the gourd rattle is reserved for women, but not exclusively. For example, in one-string fiddle ensembles in Dagomba, both men and women play the rattle simultaneously. In Wolof country, "custom demands that the women ask permission to play their instruments [reference is being made to gourd rattles] before doing so. Instruments are considered to belong to the devil, and young girls and widows are not allowed to play them lest they bring down on themselves the devil's vengeance" (Nikiprowetzky 1963: 81).

Hausa women play the largest variety of instruments, including some from all four classifications. Idiophones are the most numerous. Persons of either sex play the jew's harp (bambaro), all sorts of rattles (among them acikoko and barancaki), and calabash drums (kwarya), while such instruments as iron hand-clappers (sambani), stamping tubes (shantu), and wooden mortars (turmi) are believed to be reserved exclusively for women. Some of these instruments are performed simply for personal enjoyment—for example, the jew's harp and rattles. Two or three calabash drums, in an ensemble, accompany singing at bori rituals, wedding feasts, and other festive occasions. Iron clappers most often accompany songs of a religious nature at such occasions as weddings or naming ceremonies, religious holidays, and on eclipses of the sun (Ames and

King 1971: 10). The *shantu* is used "for social comment (for example, by a co-wife in criticism of her partners) or for informal music-making" (Ames and King 1971: 11). As accompaniment to work songs, women often rhythmically pound foodstuffs.

In Hausa society, membranophones and aerophones are very prestigious. It is usually a membranophone player who is the head of the Emir's court musicians. In addition, musicians who play wind instruments—*kakaki* and *alghaita*—are held in high regard because they record and play historical and genealogical songs about the royal family. For a woman to play such instruments is extremely rare. Ames (1973: 135), however, makes note of "women playing instruments ordinarily played by male court musicians, for example, the *taushi* [a large single membrane one-shaped drum] and the *alghaita* [a double reed pipe]." There is also evidence of women playing the *kwairama* (another type of drum) at non-courtly events (Ames 1973: 140).

As among the Tuareg, women in Hausa society are well known for playing string instruments. (These instruments, however, do not have high status in Hausaland, as I will discuss later.) The *kukuma*, a one-string fiddle, is used as a solo instrument to accompany songs at political rallies. The *kuntigi*, a single-string plucked lute, has much wider usage. It is played by men and, less often, by women to accompany songs of entertainment, politics, and praise (Ames and King 1971: 46).

We can conclude from these observations, then, that the idiophone is most widely played by women in Sudanic Africa, while the aerophone is used least. The reason for this is that idiophones have less status and significance in the ethnic groups than the drum, string, and wind instruments; and since women, with the exception of the Tuareg, do not play a dominant role in the more important institutions in society—for example, they are not the political or religious leaders, they are not the major producers of food and in no way control the economy, and they do not own property—it has probably been established that they also should not assume leadership in the performance of prominent musical instruments. Even in Hausa society, where women have the opportunity to play a wider variety of instruments, it is the exception rather than the norm for women to play aerophones and membranophones. These are ordinarily reserved for men.

Tuareg women, on the other hand, have a very high status in the culture; as a result, their participation in musical activities overshadows that of men and they, exclusively, play the more prestigious drums and strings. The only wind instrument used in the culture is played by males of the servant caste. In this case, the aerophone obviously does not have high status; if it did, it would probably be reserved for women.

Types of Performing Groups

There are several different types of women's performing groups in Sudanic Africa. At festivities performed in the privacy of their homes, women take on all roles; however, when women participate in public music-making, they generally serve either as vocal leaders or as members of the chorus, while men perform instrumental accompaniment. This division of labor does not apply among the Tuareg. In that society, female performance groups take on all roles. They are the vocal leaders, members of the chorus, *and* instrumentalists.

The second type of performance group most often found among the Tuareg consists of a male vocalist and a female instrumentalist. Usually, love songs are performed in this manner. In Tuareg society none of the songs sung by women features mordents or shakes, whereas songs performed by men invariably contain these ornamentations. According to Holiday (1956: 50-51), this is indicative of Arab influence. The women's singing style is, instead, very similar to that of sedentary groups south of the Sahara.

The Malinke prefer to use a female soloist and male instrumentalist(s). The next most likely combinations by Malinke groups are (1) male and female duets with male instrumental accompaniment or (2) female lead singers and choruses with men playing instruments.

Among the Wolof, no general preference seems apparent from the available data. Female musicians perform equally in one of three ways: (1) female soloist and no accompaniment, (2) female leader and chorus with male instrumental accompaniment, and (3) mixed vocal groups with male instrumentalists.

When women participate in Hausa music activities, they either take full responsibility for the performance of all parts or accompany men in the singing of the chorus. In Dagbon, while men take on string and drum instrumental accompaniment, women play rattles, accompany men in singing the chorus, and sometimes lead in praise singing.

Social Organization

Having considered the functions of music, the musical instruments, and the types of performing groups, let us now look at the social organization of female musicians. Are they professionals? How are they recruited and trained? What sociocultural roles and status do they have?

Most women in Sudanic Africa are nonprofessional musicians— that is, their primary source of livelihood is not performing music. These women perform music spontaneously for personal enjoyment, not for acknowledgment from the community. What occurs in Hausaland gives a good indication of what probably takes place throughout Sudanic Africa. Ames states:

Among nonprofessionals, women of all ages more often perform music than men. Married women frequently sing inside the compound, particularly when they are grinding corn or just for their own pleasure after the evening meal is finished (for example, *Shantu* music), and sometimes at wedding or naming feasts. This singing (and dancing too) is often accompanied by one of several calabash "drums" or by a hand-clapping chorus. However, it should be stressed that these performances do not take place in public, only in the inner compound . . . where the wives stay. (Ames 1973: 133)

Nonprofessional, unmarried females, such as young girls and some harlots, are less restricted in their music-making because they are not bound by the rules of *purdah* (seclusion). Harlots in Hausaland dance in public and perform on the fiddle (*kukuma*) in their rooms for clients. Young unmarried Hausa girls also dance and sing in public right up until they marry. Often, they dance outside the entrance to compounds where a naming or wedding ceremony is being held or they dance out in the streets. Male professional drummers provide the instrumental and vocal accompaniment. In the evening, the women sometimes also dance and sing inside the compound. In those instances, married women may join in by leading or responding to the singing.

Some women become professional singers as a result of their marriage to men who choose music as an occupation. This particular type of relationship is most common in Malinke, Wolof, Hausa, and, to some extent, Dagomba societies. Among the Tuareg, there are no groups of musicians who regard themselves as "professionals." According to Nikiprowetzky (1966: 55), "there are no professional musicians, as such among the Tuareg. Some blacksmiths or servants sometimes benefit from their talents as singers, but this is exceptional" (author's translation from the French). Even though Tuareg women are solely responsible for the perpetuation of musical traditions, they receive no monetary rewards for their work. Perpetuating the tradition is simply one of the duties they are expected to perform as members of the culture.

In Dabgon, the situation is different. Wives of the *lunsi* (hourglass drummers) accompany the men in singing praise and war songs at feasts (Kinney 1970: 262-263), thus gaining professional status. Where there is a *gondze* (one-string fiddle) professional, it is not the marriage partner who becomes a professional, but the offspring. Wives of *gondze* musicians are at no time allowed to perform music with the group. It is also noteworthy that regardless of the marriage situation, among the Dagomba as well as the Malinke, Wolof, and Hausa, siblings are expected to continue in the profession of their parents.

We can conclude, then, that most women in Sudanic Africa enter the music profession as a result of marriage or birth. Women who are wives of professional music-makers most often become singers in their husbands' bands. It is rare that they are allowed to perform the more highly valued instruments, but exceptions have been made, such as in Hausaland where women are known to have played instruments ordinarily reserved for male court musicians. Also, some professional married female musicians in Hausaland become ambitious and form their own groups—performing at women's feasts.

A few females *achieve* professional status on their own. Some harlots, for example, because of the substantial sums of money they are able to amass decide to become professional musicians through personal achievement. They are most commonly accepted as performers for *bori* rituals as for their clientele in harlot houses.

It is doubtful that any of the female musicians receive formal training in music. What Ames has learned about musical training among the Hausa probably also holds true in the other ethnic groups:

. . . three out of four [Hausa males] received formal instruction, and much higher percentages were recorded for the most numerous types of musicians, like recreation drummers for the youth, court musicians of all kinds and drummers for farmers. Only female singers (zabiya) were more often self-taught than not. (Ames 1968: 84)

As women associate with and accompany professional male performers, they probably learn melodies and the texts of songs through imitation. Formal training is not necessary to play musical instruments such as rattles and scrapers, for the performance technique is not as difficult as that for some drum, wind, and string instruments. Whether Tuareg women formally teach other females some of the techniques for playing the imzad, tinde, and water drums is not known. We can assume, however, that since Tuareg women devote much of their time to fine art accomplishments, they also make an effort to ensure that they are knowledgeable in playing musical instruments properly.

In some Sudanic cultures neither female nor male musicians are highly respected. One of the reasons nonmusicians do not want or allow their daughters to marry musicians is because the musician's occupational group is ranked so low. This particular situation is very much the case in Malinke, Wolof, and Hausa societies. In contrast, among the Tuareg and Dagomba, where the music profession is a symbol of prestige rather than degradation, females consider musicians to be attractive marriage partners.

Let us look more closely at the situation in each society. Among the Tuareg, since females already have high status, regardless of whether they are professional or nonprofessional musicians, it just follows suit that the same high status is given to their music-making. Moreover, these women are the primary carriers of the society's important musical traditions.

In Malinke and Wolof cultures, musicians are both admired and despised. On the one hand, "as historians and genealogists they are the storehouses of the records of a country that has disdained the written language; as musicians, they are present at festive and solemn occasions alike" (Nikiprowetzky 1963: 79). On the other hand the musician's caste, like that of the blacksmiths, the rope-makers, and the weavers, is one of the lowest in the hierarchy. Further, musicians invite more disdain because they have the power to build or destroy a person's reputation in the community since they know a good deal about many individuals' family histories. They can always use or even invent damaging information to elicit more pay for their services. Musicians in Senegal arouse feelings of fear and contempt to such a degree that in certain parts of the country, according to Nikiprowetzky (1963: 79), "griots [musicians] do not even have the right to burial; for it is said that earth in which a griot has been laid will be sterile forever, or at least that its fertility will diminish year by year. Their mortal remains are placed instead inside a crooked *baobab* tree."

In Hausaland, although the status of all musicians is rather low, some are ranked higher than others, depending upon whom they patronize and the type of music they perform or instrument they play. Musicians attached to a royal court or officialdom are more highly respected than those who do not have these positions. On the other hand, performers who play for *bori* rituals have a very low status. In addition, membranophone and aerophone players, even those not attached to the Emir's court, have a higher status than musicians who play string instruments. The primary reason for the differentiation in status is Islamic influence. In pre-Islamic Arabia, it was thought that the *jinn* (a spiritual being) and the spirit world could be called up through music; it was claimed that some music was derived from the *jinn* and even *shaitan* (Satan) himself (Anderson 1971: 146). This attitude caused so much controversy that Muslim leaders changed this position and began to accept certain kinds of music-making. Still, even when singing and other instrumental types were partially accepted by adherents to Islam, string instruments were (and still often are) excluded because of their connection to metaphysical elements (DjeDje 1978: 34-35).

Thus, professional female musicians who play string instruments have an extremely low status. In addition, females are famous for their *bori* performances and, as mentioned, these have low status. That some Hausa women entertain clients in harlot houses is another factor that contributes to their low status.

Most drum, wind, and string players in Dagbon are thought of very highly. To be a *gondze* (one-string fiddler) in Dagbon, for example, is a highly respected honor. Fiddling is also a well-paid profession within Dagomba culture. Fiddlers are recognized by the king and the community as part of the royal family and accorded certain privileges.[7] Thus, in Dagomba culture, in contrast to Malinke, Wolof, and Hausa cultures, females pursue male musicians as likely marriage partners.

Nonprofessional female musicians are not looked upon as important contributors to music-making. Most of their performances are for the purpose of entertaining themselves rather than the public. As a result, community members do not even know the musical capability of these females. It is, therefore, difficult to identify a status and sociocultural value for them. On the one hand, people have no reason to fear them because they do not spread harmful rumors through their singing; on the other hand, they do not record important history nor are they attached to the king or other important officials. Presumably, they are regarded as "second-class" individuals, mirroring their overall position in the society.

CONCLUSION

Early influences in the Sudan, in particular the Arabic, provide the historical and cultural backdrop with which to understand the role of women in music among the Taureg, Malinke, Wolof, Hausa, and Dagomba. The material presented leads us to conclude that Arabic/Islamic culture has had a tremendous impact on traditional Sudanic society. As a result of foreign intervention, women are now excluded from many segments of life where they were previously accepted as equals. For example, it was formerly not uncommon for women to participate fully in traditional religious practices; become involved equally with men in economic pursuits such as agriculture and animal husbandry; and appear at public occasions. Now, women are expected to dispense with such activities.

Female involvement in musical activities reflects these changes in social status. We cannot, however, dismiss the possibility that these societies differentiated primary and secondary roles for men and women in music. Perhaps some of the societies in the savannah belt who appear to have adopted foreign elements—especially musical traditions—were already practicing similar customs even before Arab practices were introduced into the area. Still, the fact that women have a very high status among the Tuareg and are almost totally responsible for the continuity of music in the culture demonstrates that the acculturation process can be selective; only features that are complimentary or beneficial to a people in their particular situation need be accepted. Contrary to the Malinke, Wolof, Hausa, and Dagomba, the Tuareg are monogamous and have a matrilineal system of inheritance. In this, the Tuareg differ sharply from their Berber kinsmen, Arab conquerors, and other Sudanic peoples.

Regardless of what actually happened during the acculturation process between Africans and Arabs, it can still be concluded that a woman's sociocultural status correlates with her role and position in musical activities. Further, information presented in this study reveals that the condition of women in the Sudan is not very different from that of women in other cultures throughout the world, particularly those in the West. That is, only when women are respected and given equal partnership in religious, economic, social, and political institutions, will they be equal participants in the musical culture.

NOTES

1. The research in West Africa was made possible through a doctoral fellowship from the Ford Foundation.

2. The terms Sudanic, Sudan, and savannah belt will be used interchangeably.

3. Countries in West Africa include the following: Mauritania, Senegal, the Gambia, Mali, Guinea, Guinea Bissau, Sierra Leone, Liberia, Ivory Coast, Ghana, Burkina Faso, Niger, Togo, Benin, Nigeria, and the Cameroon.

4. The Western Sudan stretches approximately from 18° West Longitude to 2° West Longitude, while the Central Sudan comprises that area from 2° West Longitude to 18° East Longitude.

5. The Tukulor were a group of people who lived in Mauritania until they migrated eastwards; they are believed to be related to the Fulani (Fulbe).

6. Some Muslims in Nobere, especially those who have been to Mecca, have started to place their wives in. a kind of *purdah* (the seclusion of women from public observation). For example, they refuse to permit their

wives to go to market for fear they will come into contact with "ungodly" pagan men (Skinner 1966: 366-367).

7. For further discussion see DjeDje (1978: 221).

REFERENCES

Ames, David. 1959. "Wolof co-operative work groups." In *Continuity and Change in African Cultures*, ed. William R. Bascom and Melville J. Herskovits. Chicago: University of Chicago Press.

————. 1968. "The musicians of Zaria and Obimo." *African Arts* 1.

————. 1973. "A sociocultural view of Hausa musical activity." In *The Traditional Artist in African Societies*, ed. Warren L. D'Azevedo. Bloomington: Indiana University Press.

Ames, David, and Anthony King. 1971. *Glossary of Hausa Music and Its Social Contexts*. Evanston: Northwestern University Press.

Ames, David W., and Ken A. Gourlay. 1978. "Kimkim: A women's musical pot," *African Arts* 11.

Anderson, Lois. 1971. "The Interrelation of African and Arab Musics: Some preliminary considerations." In *Essays on Music and History in Africa*, ed. Klaus Wachsmann. Evanston: Northwestern University Press, 143-169.

Aryee, Enoch. 1973. Adaawe: A study of game songs of the Ga women folk. M.A. thesis, University of California, Los Angeles.

Ballandier, Georges. 1948. "Femmes possedes et leur chants," *Presence Africaine* 5.

Bebey, Francis. 1975. *African Music: A People's Art*. Trans. from the French by Josephine Bennett. New York: Lawrence Hill and Co.

Blacking, John. 1969. "Songs, dances, mimes, and symbolism of Venda girls' initiation schools," *African Studies* 28.

Carlisle, Roxane Connick. 1975. "Women singers in Darfur, Sudan Republic." *The Black Perspective in Music* 3.

Cutter, Charles. 1968. "The politics of music in Mali." *African Arts* 1.

Djedje, Jacqueline Cogdell. 1978. "The One String Fiddle in West Africa: A Comparison of Hausa and Dagomba Traditions." Ph.D. dissertation. Los Angeles: University of California.

Drinker, Sophie. 1948. *Music and Women: The Story of Women in Their Relation to Music*. Washington, D.C.: Zenger Publishing Co.

Dupire, Marguerite. 1973. "Women in a pastoral society." In *Peoples and Cultures of Africa*, ed. Elliott P. Skinner. Garden City, N.Y.: Doubleday Natural History Press.

Farmer, Henry. 1939. "Early references to music in the Western Sudan."

Journal of the Royal Asiatic Society.

Foedermayer, Franz. 1966-67. "The Arabian influence in the Tuareg music." *African Music* 4.

Gunner, Elizabeth. 1979. "Songs of innocence and experience: Women as composers and performers of (*izibongo*) Zulu praise poetry," *Research in African Literatures* 10.

Holiday, Geoffrey. 1956. "The Tuareg of the Ahaggar." *African Music* 1.

Hollis, A.C. 1924. "Dance of Sagara women, Tanganyika Territory," *Man* 24.

Johnston, Thomas F. 1976. "Secret rites of the Tsonga girls' initiation (Khomba)" *Papers in Anthropology* 17.

————. 1978. "Conflict resolution in Tsonga co-wifely jealousy songs," *Africana Marburgensia* 11.

Kinney, Sylvia. 1970. "Drummers in Dagbon: The role of the drummer in the Dagomba Festival." *Ethnomusicology* 14.

Laye, Camara. 1954. *The Dark Child.* New York: Farrar, Straus and Giroux.

Lewis, I. M., ed. 1966. *Islam in Tropical Africa: Studies Presented and Discussed at the Fifth International African Seminar, Ahmadu Bello University, Zaria, January 1964.* London: Oxford University Press.

Luneau, René. 1981. *Chants de femmes au Mali.* Paris: Luneau Ascot.

Merriam, Alan P. 1970. *African Music on LP: An Annotated Discography.* Evanston: Northwestern University Press.

Murdock, George P. 1959. *Africa: Its Peoples and Their Culture History.* New York: McGraw Hill Book Co.

Nikiprowetzky, Tolia. 1963. "The griots of Senegal and their instruments." *Journal of the International Folk Music Council* 15.

————. 1964. "L'ornamentation dans la musique des Touareg de l'Air." *Journal of the International Folk Music Council* 16.

————. 1966. "Musical instruments in the Niger." In *Trois Aspets de la Musique Africaine: Mauritanic, Senegal, Niger.* Paris: Office de Cooperation Radiophonique.

Nketia, J. H. Kwabena. 1974. *The Music of Africa.* New York: W. W. Norton and Co., Inc.

Obichere, Boniface I. 1971. *West African States and European Expansion: The Dahomey-Nigher Hinterland, 1885-1898.* New Haven and London: Yale University Press.

Oppong, Christine. 1973. *Growing Up in Dagbon.* Accra-Tema, Ghana: Ghana Publishing Corp.

Ottenberg, Phoebe V. 1959. "The changing economic position of women among the Afikpo Ibo." In *Continuity and Change in African Cultures,* ed. William R. Bascom and Melville Herskovits. Chicago: University of Chicago Press.

Rouch, Jean. 1954. Notes on Migrations into the Gold Coast (First report of the mission carried out in the Gold Coast from March to December 1954), trans. by O.E.O. and J. B. Heigham. Accra, Ghana.

Skinner, Elliott P. 1966. "Islam in Mossi society." In *Islam in Tropical Africa*, ed. I. M. Lewis. London: Oxford University Press.

Smith, M. G. 1965. "The Hausa of Northern Nigeria." In *Peoples of Africa*, ed. James L. Gibbs, Jr. New York: Holt, Rinehart and Winston, Inc.

Stenning, Derrick, J. 1965. "The pastoral Fulani of Northern Nigeria." In *Peoples of Africa*, ed. James L. Gibbs, Jr. New York: Holt, Rinehart, and Winston, Inc.

Strobel, Margaret. 1975. "Women's wedding celebrations in Mombasa, Kenya." *African Studies Review* 18.

Trimingham, J. S. 1962. *A History of Islam in West Africa*. London: Oxford University Press.

Twala, Regina G. 1952. "Umblanga (reed) ceremony of the Swazi maidens," *African Studies* 11.

White, C.M.N. 1953. "Conservatism and modern adaptation in Luvale female puberty ritual," *Africa* 23.

Music and Dance Guilds
in Igede

DEMOGRAPHY, ETHNICITY AND
SOCIO-CULTURAL FEATURES

The Igede of Nigeria have a population today of approximately
180,000.[1] They occupy over 1,000 square miles on the southern
edge of Benue State bordering Anambra State at the southwest and
Cross River State at the southeast (see figure 7.1). They occupy Oju
Local Government Area, which used to be part of the old Idoma
division and later Otukpo division, but attained its own divisional
status in February 1976, following the country-wide split of former
states and divisions. Since the early thirties they have been grouped
together with their neighbors the Idoma for administrative purposes and have accepted the designation of Idoma to the extent that
the current *Och' Idoma*, the paramount chief of Idoma, is from
Igede. The Idoma are one of the principal ethnic groups in Benue
State, and Otukpo town, the administrative seat of the whole
Idoma territory (including Oju division), is about thirty-six miles to
the northwest of Central Igede. While there is some cultural overlapping, the Igede's history, language, and culture are distinct from
that of the Idoma.

Since Oju L.G.A. borders on the northern edge of the equatorial
forests of central Africa, the area has many trees and contains some hills and valleys—ripples from the vast backbone of
the Cameroon Highlands some 130 miles to the southeast. "Most of

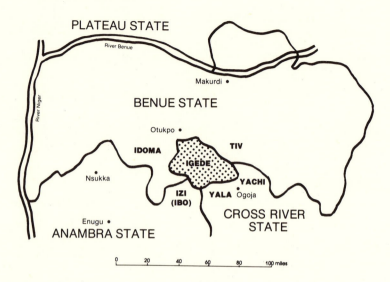

Figure 7.1 The location of Igede and neighboring ethnic groups

the Igede are farmers, produce such crops as yams, cassava, maize, beniseed, millet, and guinea corn. Typically they live in scattered villages or hamlets in houses built of sun-baked mud, roofed with thatch" (Anon. 1980: 1).

I first arrived in Igede on a Christmas Eve. A friend, the nephew of Chief J. I. Idikwu, the District Head of Igede, had invited me to spend the Christmas period with the Idikwu family in his uncle's compound. During that initial visit I found that, in Igede, Christmas is primarily a time to relax with family and friends. Although Christianity has been adopted widely in Igede, the commercial trappings and folk customs associated with Christmas in the Western World have made little impact. The dominant impressions of that time relate to the natural environment, the gentle power of the red Igede earth, the rolling hills and clumps of thick forest. These remain distinct in my memory. There was a memorable Igede hymn, sung by a group of carol singers as they toured the streets beneath the palms, and a full moon on Christmas Eve. But the richness of the Igede musical heritage remained for me as yet unknown and unsuspected until the following September when I returned for *Iged'agba*—the New Yam Festival.

There is nothing haphazard about the timing for traditional Igede music and dance. Occasions are prescribed by convention and little musical activity—with the exception of the informal music of the compound—takes place outside a framework of music associations.

Particular occasions of the life cycle or the yearly cycle call for celebration with music and dance. The nature of the occasion, in turn, determines the nature of the music. When a member of a dance guild takes a new wife or acquires a new house, or after a heavy period of farm labor, are, for example, occasions for music and dance. Or when a newly formed guild chooses a patron or composes a new song and wants to test public reaction, these too are occasions for music and dance. Recently, music has become an ingredient of the agricultural shows, political rallies, and visits of various dignitaries. Unlike other African peoples, the Igede do not mix music or dance with work. There are no Igede work-songs and neither collective farmwork nor domestic activities are accompanied by any songs or synchronized group movements. "When you work, you work; when you sing, you sing," Ikape Arubi, the *Ayidewoh* (master dancer) of *Andibla*, informed me. The dances that accompany the stirring "music of war" (*ayilo nya ewu*) and "music of hunting" (*ayilo nya urweh*), while vigorous and passionate, have no obvious pantomimic movements. The heritage of formalized music associations has possibly resulted from the distinction made between music and other activities.

Within Igede, funeral ceremonies are by far the most significant of the life-cycle rituals and music and dance performance are an integral part. The music connected with funerals is the most profound in the Igede repertoire. When the ancestors mingle with the living in the meeting ground (*ojiya*), the full force of tradition can be observed.

While traditionally the Igede wove their own cloth, constructed pots, worked in iron, and carved statues, the height of Igede artistic endeavor reveals itself in the people's music and dance and the paraphernalia that are a most important component. Of this art they are justifiably proud, for in carving masks, weaving costumes, and making other decorations for musical performances, Igede visual art reaches a peak.

A large proportion of the population is involved to some degree in traditional musical activities, despite the impact of transistor radios and commercial records. There is nothing coincidental about this, for in Igede, as in other Nigerian communities, the art of music and dance has been deliberately cultivated for its social benefit.

Apart from games of an intellectual nature, adults in Igede traditionally have no recreational sport. Thus, music and dance are the major recreation, satisfying social, aesthetic, and competitive instincts. Each village has its music association(s) or dance guilds, and an adult male will typically belong to at least one. Some villages have as many as four guilds. Music and dance are a source of both individual pleasure and communal pride. A skillful music association can win prestige and popularity for the entire village.

My study was confined to Central Igede District. Unfortunately, limitations of time and poor transportation facilities made it impossible for me to observe all the music associations of the Igede. I did, however, document the musical activities of the "conventional" guilds—that is, those whose structure predominated in Oju L.G.A. meaning that they had masquerades attached to them and appeared principally at funerals. These included the *Ogirinye*, the *Onyantu*, the *Ijege*, and the *Aitah* (Nicholls 1984: 70-76). Another guild, the *Etuh*, was distinctive in that its song lyrics, delivered in the form of prophetic proverbs, were the focal point of the guild's musical activities. *Etuh* does not participate in funeral celebrations as its primary function is recreational. (By contrast, some music guilds performed publicly only at the funeral of one of their members, see figure 7.2.) *Abwo* was the only example I documented of a traditional adult women's organization. With the help of Chief Idikwu and his family, I eventually came to understand the important role dance guilds play in Igede life.

Cultural Grouping

From consulting Herskovits' (1948) culture area map of Africa, it appears that the Igede border three powerful culture areas—the Guinea Coast to the west, the Western Sudan to the north, and the Congo Area to the southeast. In many aspects of Igede life, the Congo influence seems to predominate, and Igede music displays many features that are characteristic of the equatorial forest regions from the Cameroons through the Congo.

If we adopt the categories of K. A. Gourlay (1979), who divides

Figure 7.2 The *Etuh* Musical Association of Adum Owo (R. Nicholls)

Nigeria into four music areas, Igede falls within the "Bar Zither-Slit Gong Area" or simply the "Slit-Gong Area," since the Bar Zither is in the process of disappearing from some groups. This area includes the southern part of Gongola State, the whole of Benue, Bendel, Anambra, Imo, and Rivers States, and part of Cross River State. As the slit-gong (*ogirigboh*) reproduces the tones and speech patterns of the local language, it significantly shapes the Igede musical form, both in rhythm pattern and in melody line. Although the musical instruments of one tribal group are very seldom found intact in another group, the *ogirigboh*, metal gongs, wickerwork maracas, and single-headed membranophone drums appear almost invariably throughout the area. The *ogumh* (thumb piano) is found universally throughout Africa.

The style of vocal polyphony is characteristic throughout this section of Nigeria;[2] however, also in evidence in older Igede music is the interlocking choral technique, which reaches eminence in the "hocketing" style of the pygmies of the Ituri forest, in which single notes or musical segments are repeated in rotation by individual vocalists, creating a choral background over which the lead singer traces the melody line.[3] The style is apparent in some traditional Idoma recordings, notably that of Madam Onyebe Adeka and her Aja Group from Otukpo township.

This musical diffusion over vast areas is not surprising since the Igede share many religious traditions with their neighbors. For example, the celebration of the New Yam Festival is common to the whole area southeast of the Niger-Benue confluence. In addition, throughout the area, funerals are a dominant life-cycle ritual. A further example of shared culture is the presence of warrior societies and the practice—traditionally—of presenting a human skull at the funeral of a noted warrior. In the past, in order to join Igede's *Ogirinye* warrior association (shared by the Iyala and the Idoma), an Igede had to have killed a foe in combat and collected his skull. This made him a "man." Among the Ibo of Bende division in Imo State, the *Ikpirikpe* warrior association served a similar function. This practice occurred in Cross River State also. Even the Tiv, who in many cultural aspects have remained distinct, traditionally buried their warriors with skulls.[4]

In addition to the shared cultural traditions, which eases the exchange of music, there is another factor: new styles of music and dance transverse ethnic boundaries rather easily—especially between the Igede and the Iyala and Idoma—because the Igede intermarry with these groups to a certain extent. In general, music tends to spread through the channels of communication created by affinal bonds. The Igede masquerade associations, the *Onyantu* and *Ijege*, for example, are of Iyala origin and their songs are still sung in the Iyala language. Similarly, the people of Ito, a village near to the Otukpo boundary, adopted from the neighboring Idoma the *Anjenu* possession cult in which superhuman feats are performed.

Traditional Religious Beliefs

Common to virtually all traditional African religions is the concept of an impersonal, supreme god who, although the creator of the universe, is remote from man and indifferent to his daily affairs. In Igede society this god is called *Ohe-Oluhye* (god above) and depicted as clear, blue sky. The supreme god, too vast to be worshipped directly, is approached through an intermediary, a lesser god named *Ohe-Ogbadogogo*. A canalization of spiritual power, he assures man of the supreme god's benevolence. *Ohe-Ogbadogogo* dwells within the *Ubwo* fig tree, which is planted in the compound. In a society that gives childbearing and fertility paramount importance, it is not surprising to find that an extremely prolific and durable tree such as the *ubwo* represents the beneficial power of the supreme god.

It should be noted, though, that in addition to the "good" *Ohe-Ogbadogogo* there is also *Ohe-Onyobi*, a "bad" god who is represented by an *ubwo* tree, an *unwu* (kapok) tree, and an *ugbwilebwu* tree, planted together and living in a symbiotic relationship with each other. "*Onyobi*" in Igede language means "evil," and bad luck or unsuccessful ventures may be attributed to *Ohe-Onyobi*. This grouping of trees is planted away from the compound and is placated in times of misfortune.[5]

Another dominant concept the Igede share with the majority of African peoples is the preeminence of the ancestors in spiritual and political life. The ancestors (*Alegwu-Ale-eji*) are perceived to be corporate spirits, intermediaries between God and man. In the broadest sense, the term "ancestors" describes all the myriads of psyches of all those who have lived and died—the corporate body *en masse*. The ancestors tend to merge with, or have a specific relationship to, the Spirit of the Earth (*Ohe-Oleji*).

At a more concrete level, the ancestors of a lineage have a vested interest in perpetuating their lineage. They are considered to be omnipresent, continually watching over their kindred and influencing their lives. "Living and dead of the same lineage are in a permanent relationship with each other. . . . The living act as temporary caretakers of the prosperity, prestige and general well-being of the lineage, on behalf of the ancestors who did the same during their lives" (Middleton 1960: 25).

Among the Igede, the corporate spirits of the dead are thought to reside in the earth below. They are next in rank to *Ohe-Oluhye*, the supreme god in the sky above.

Man was thus placed between two powers or forces—that of the Sky god and that of the Earth god. . . . The individual had to worship both powers—the one above and the one beneath. Ohe-Oluhye was regarded as the supreme power or god, but in the event of an impending punishment from him. Alegwu-Aleji (the corporate spirits of the dead) or Ohe-Oleji could be appealed to so that they, representing the power beneath, could plead to the power above for the living (Okita 1973: 19).

With prayer and sacrifice to a shrine of stones, placed at the foot of *Ohe-Ogbadogogo*, the head of a family could communicate both with the supreme god (during morning devotions) and with the ancestors (in the evening).

The traditional Igede concept of time is circular; the subjective "now" lies in the center, and the past and future radiate from this point. The Igede believe in reincarnation and say they are quite often born among their mother's agnates and daughters' descendants. (Circle dances featured during the Igede funeral ceremony possibly depict this circular view of time.)[6]

The ancestors, although behind the living in time, have, in fact, trodden the same path before those who live in the present; thus they are also ahead of them, affecting and influencing their everyday affairs. "In the everyday speech of Igede that which you cherish and respect as being of the ancestors is also referred to as being of the dawn or the morning" (Ranung 1973). Music and dance is thought of as an inheritance from the forefathers, and traditional music is called "music of the dawn." Dawn, when the day begins, is connected with renewal and, by extension, creativity. The ancestors are believed to be concerned not only with the continuity and conservation of tradition, but also with regenerative and creative aspects.[7]

The authority of the ancestors is passed into the human realm with the power vested in *Achuku*, the Igede ancestor society, comprised of the adult men of the village. *Achuku* is the final instrument of sociopolitical control, since traditional Igede society lacks any centralized authority, resembling the segmentary acephalous structure of Ibo society. *Achuku*'s decisions have divine authority since members of *Achuku* are responsible for the communities' relationships with the ancestors. The *Achuku* assembly elects a headman, the *Ogabwo*, who is the oldest and most revered man in the village. He controls all communal shrines and is charged with the custody of the sacred *Achuku* drum, which summons the souls of the dead to the village to witness the activities of the *Achuku* society.

The *Achuku* shrine occupies a special place in the village meeting ground and is set apart from the earth shrine of the village and the shrines of the collective guardian spirits. There is also a special roped-off area that is reserved for the *Achuku* meetings, whose deliberations are kept a strict secret. Women and children are forbidden to see *Achuku* meetings in session. While music and dance do not play a major role in *Achuku*, music of a secret nature (*ayilo ibaa*) is performed when new members are accepted into the group or when the group commemorates an old member's death.

The female counterpart for *Achuku* is *Imwo*. This society's main function is to regulate female conduct and protect the interests of both its members and all the females in Igede society as a whole. *Imwo* performs publicly as a principal means of expressing social criticism. The pointed and biting satire contained in the lyrics regulates the conduct of overzealous males.

TRADITIONAL MUSIC AND DANCE

Adult Music Associations

Although the Igede word *"ewoh"* signifies "dance," there is no word in Igede that strictly refers to music as separate from dance.

The term *"Ayilo"* denotes a complex of song, instrumental music, and choreographic movements and each music association is formed around such an *ayilo* complex. The final combination of song, instrumental accompaniment, and dance distinguishes one type of music from another.

A music type with its corresponding association generally originates as the inspiration of a single composer, who will initially own the music. He is the *Ongodomu*—"the one who started it." While the *Ongodomu* is responsible for the name and form of the music, he *and* his fellow guild members will be responsible for its development. If the music type proves to have lasting popular appeal, it will, after a period of elaboration, expansion, and standardization, be established as a definitive form. It will then be characterized by a certain combination of instruments, adhering to a set rhythmic design; established song texts with specified, responsorial relations between soloists and choir; a dance pattern of more or less marked choreographic complexity; and possibly one or two masquerade costumes, worn by expert dancers on special occasions—notably, funerals (Ranung 1973). A music type spawns a music association in that the association will be formed around, and named after, the music type. The association will perform only music and dance that correspond to the specific music type. This restriction in no way limits individual musicians; a talented musician may belong to more than one association.

Some types of music are very localized: the *Etuh* guild, for example, exists in only one village and the *Ongodumu*, Odeh Egbang, is still active within the association. *Ogirinye*, on the other hand, is deeply rooted in many parts of Benue State and the originator has long since been forgotten.

Each music association has a particular music station, *ega nya ayilo*, set within the village meeting ground (or playground as it is affectionately known). Typically located near the periphery, it is simply a small clearing amid the trees, with an open end facing the meeting ground's spacious center. Although the dance activities may utilize the whole of the meeting ground arena, the music association will set up the instruments at, and base its performance from, the music station. It is common for charms—that protect the music—to be buried there.

Throughout Igede history, many music associations have come into prominence, declined, and been forgotten. Many were associated with warfare, the music designed to stir the blood and raise the adrenalin level; however, with the termination of institutionalized warfare, the intense and violent music of war has lost some of its exalted status. Gradually, the various, diverse warrior masquerades of the past are being absorbed into the all-embracing *Aitah*. As a consequence, *Aitah* masquerades vary significantly among the various clans of Igede. The *Aitah* masquerades that I documented from the Ibilla clan, for example, showed markedly different characteristics from the *Aitah* of Oju, although the music styles are compatible (see figures 7.3 and 7.4). An Igede elder who has been active in communal affairs will be able to list many forgotten music guilds, along with the different masquerades he has witnessed. The remnants of music stations long past can be discovered in overgrown, neglected areas at the fringes of the meeting grounds.

In Igede most music associations do not restrict their membership to males or females. Even the traditional warrior associations would accept women who demonstrated exceptional bravery. The majority of the mixed dance groups, however, are dominated by men, and women members are neither allowed to beat drums nor wear the masquerade costume. "Anyone is free to enter a music and dance association on the condition that he in one way or other takes an active part in its doings and follows the rules jointly agreed upon. . . ." (Ranung 1973).

Musical ability is highly esteemed in Igede and composers and musicians are greatly admired and respected. Through his virtuosity, an expert performer might win the title of *ayidewoh*—master dancer—or his voice likened to the *owuna*, a song bird common in Benue State. Additionally, an outstanding performance can win a man a wife.

Participation in music is also an investment for the future among the Igede, since all the music types a person belongs to are performed at his funeral, in turn adding to its grandeur. A person can also arrange to have his guild perform at the funeral of one of his relatives.

The Igede Funeral

Igede dance guilds and music associations function primarily in the context of funeral wakes and ceremonies.

Within a society such as the Igede, in which the ancestors feature

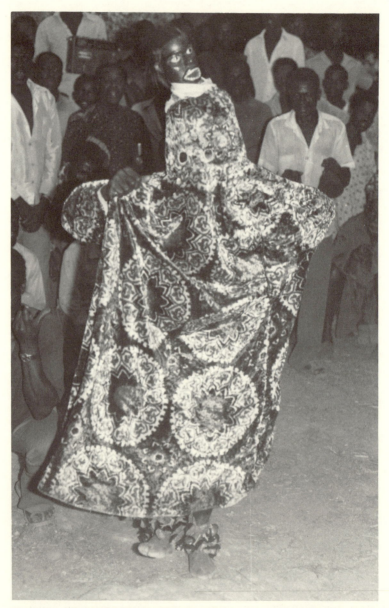

Figure 7.3 The *Aitah* "Ibelebele" masquerade of Andibla. Although worn by a male dancer, the velvet signifies a female masquerade (R. Nicholls)

so prominently, it is not surprising that the funeral should be the most elaborately celebrated occasion in communal life; after all, the funeral marks the passage of a community member into the ancestral realm. At first, it may seem odd to the western mind to associate vigorous music and dancing with the funeral process, accustomed as it is to link funerals with solemn mourning. It should be remembered, however, that a major mode of modern Western music grew out of the funeral tradition: Jazz was born in the funeral parades of New Orleans, patronized by Black and creole societies at the turn of the century.

For the Igede, dance can serve as an expression of grief and a form of tribute to the deceased. Arubi Eje, a member of the *Onyantu* association explained: "How are you going to express it when someone you love dies? Are you going to kiss his dead lips and say goodbye? You will *dance*, that is the way to express your sorrow."

The funeral ceremony (*idah*) is, however, by no means a mournful or sorrowful occasion. It is a major social event, and people are attracted by the grandeur of the occasion and the chance to witness some of the top musicians play. In a segmentary society such as the Igede, which traditionally had no formalized system of centralized government or communication, social occasions like the funeral serve a cohesive function, crucial in promoting intervillage unity and understanding. Many of the guests may not have known the deceased personally; nevertheless, they want to register solidarity with the bereaved family. Silas Okita, a native of Igede, explains:

Members of the family of the deceased were also consoled by the featuring of the dances. While the dances no doubt entertained the audience, the presence of the whole village at the playing ground for the occasion was a great mark of solidarity because apart from the entertainment, the presence of both the young and the old demonstrated their last homage to the deceased as well as demonstrating their concern for the bereaved. In fact the esteem in which a man was held when he was alive could be measured by the number of people that turned out to the playing ground to pay their last homage (Okita 1973: 3).

The amount of time and resources expended on a funeral is determined by the age, sex, and social status of the deceased. The death through old age of a respected male elder, who was connected to various guilds and lived a long and fruitful life, will demand the most elaborate funeral ceremony. Women's funerals generally elicit less ceremonial ritual; moreover, for women, the masquerade and dancing do not take place in the meeting ground as for prominent men, but in the compound of the woman's husband or father. By the same token, the funeral of a child or adolescent is not as comprehensive as that for an adult.[8]

On the day that an old man dies, the *ogirigboh* slit drum is brought to his compound. From there, the *ogirigboh* player of a guild to which the old man belonged beats out the news. Using the drum names of other guild members, he calls them to the compound. Neighbors and fellow villagers pay visits of sympathy to the compound where family members are going into mourning.

The corpse is washed and dressed in fine clothes and seated in a chair. If the deceased was a man with some status, a proven warrior or a conspicuous member of *Achuku*, his corpse is raised in a seated position on a bamboo platform (*agwurube*) outside his hut and kept there for a period of lamentation, which lasts for three days. The height of the platform depends on his status. For reasons of hygiene, a small fire is kept lit under the corpse. During the three days of lamentation, dance groups keep vigil at the side of their companion on the platform. Throughout the night, they perform music and dance until day returns and the bereaved family resume their mourning. The dancing is their means not only to express grief but to convey their comprehension of the gravity of life and death and the temporality of human existence.

In Igede, as in other African communities, the ancestors are conceptualized as intimately involved in the expression of music and dance. While the community is lamenting the loss of a loved one during the wake, the ancestors are preparing to receive his spirit. They are consequently concerned that the rites of passage, of which music and dance are an integral part, are performed in a fitting manner. The song and dance complex performed during the wake, then, is both a form of tribute to the deceased and homage to the ancestors, from whom the existing society derives existence.

Following the three-day period of lamentation the corpse is buried. Depending on the extent of the preparations for the funeral ceremony, the ceremony may or may not take place on the day of the burial. In cases where the required preparations for the funeral ceremony are many and/or many of the family members are absent from Igede, the funeral ceremony will be postponed. The time lapse can extend over several years but the funeral ceremony cannot be postponed indefinitely. Eventually, the ceremony is held.

People come from near and far, dressed in festive attire. Children are scrubbed and dressed in their best. Young men set their attention on favorably impressing the young ladies. Everybody attends with the exception of the matrons of the family—who stay in the compound to prepare for the feasting and toasting that will take place following the ceremony—and pregnant women. In common with the Asante people of Ghana, the Igede mother-to-be believes that her child's features will be affected by what she looks at while pregnant, and so she is not to observe the startling visage of the masquerade.

On the day of the funeral, the meeting ground is prepared. The deceased's mat is placed in a tree. About an hour before sunset one of the musical associations positions itself in its music station. At sunset the sound of the music draws the Igede people in ones, twos, or little groups to the *ojiya* arena. Various musical and dance events take place during the two to three hours that follow, their type depending on the musical guilds that are featured.

In addition to watching the performance of the masquerades, community members take part in the *Ewoh-ologba* circle dance or exhibit their individual skills in the *Ewoh-okpoko* solo dance. For the *Ewoh-ologba* circle dance, adult males and females form a circle and dance slowly round and round, repeating a chorus initiated by the music association. A single male dancer enters the arena by the authority of the cloth tied around his waist. The dance brings out the competitive spirit. A young man may end his performance by throwing the waist cloth at the feet of his rival, a challenge destined to bring the recipient bad luck unless resolved within the dance performance.[9]

Although children are encouraged to engage in music and dance in daily life, when the *Ogirigboh* appears in the meeting ground and the top musicians of the village gather, the children are relegated to the periphery of the arena. I saw only one child participate in an *Ewoh-okpoko* dance. A boy of about eight, with a large cloth tied around his waist, danced for less than a minute before being swept off his feet and carried aloft to the edge of the arena amid enthusiastic applause. He was described to me as "the son of the masquerade."[10]

The funeral is brought to a climax and terminated with six dances

Figure 7.4 The *Aitah* "Onyuwunyu" masquerade of Oju, dancing at a funeral. Both of the Aitah masquerades at this funeral wore rough costumes. Possibly both are considered male (R. Nicholls)

by male and female masquerades. Guided into the arena by attendants with switches of foliage, they dance alternately, three dances
each, although they will dance at least one dance together. This is
the high point in the ceremony and the masquerades' performance
brings forth roars of appreciation from the onlookers (see figure
7.4). By the time the performance is over, night has fallen; the
crowds disperse to the compound of the deceased's family, where
they are entertained with food, cola nuts, story-telling, music, and
palm wine that flows late into the night. The goats and fowls killed
for the occasion, as well as the wine and beer provided to the guests,
are, in a sense, offerings on behalf of the deceased, who is, in turn,
gratified by the heightened prestige the event affords him.

With the successful culmination of the funeral, the acceptance of
the deceased's spirit into the ancestral ranks is assured. The tension
hovering over the compound prior to the ceremony has been dis-
sipated by the masquerades' performance. The atmosphere is now
considerably relaxed. "The dance groups have in advance reserved
a place for themselves in the compound and during the night
separate dance rings will continually be formed, within which
anyone on his own initiative or by the call of his drum name may
burst into dance. Music may also accompany the sharing of beans
and palmwine. . . ."(Ranung 1973)

Throughout Igede evolutionary development, Igede musical
culture has been preserved. Even though associational life and
accompanying customs are somewhat formalized, music and
dance, preserved as they are through nonverbal means, are fluid
and fragile. As a consequence, there is nothing predetermined
about an Igede performance; its final form is determined by the
occasion, the individuals involved, the social atmosphere, and a
host of other variables. But whatever its form, a successful funeral
reaffirms the communities' traditional values and perception of
existence.

Music of the Compound

The music that emanates from an Igede compound is mostly of
an informal nature, made by family members or visiting friends. It
may be a part of another event, such as the recitation of oral narra-
tives; it may have a specific function as the lullaby does; or, par-

ticularly for the very old or the very young, it may simply be a source of amusement. On some evenings, especially during the dry season when the pressure of farm work is less, families gather to listen to the folktales of the elders. These tales, in addition to being entertaining, contain a lesson in social behavior or a moral of some sort. The audience participates by joining in songs and poems, repeating stanzas, designed to make the experience more memorable. Musical mnemonic devices are part of the African tradition and a large part of Igede oral history was originally preserved in songs or poems. When questioned on obscure Igede history, an elder may resort to singing softly to himself in order to clarify the details.

Elderly people who have fewer chores than more youthful folk may amuse themselves by reminiscing through song, singing the old songs, possibly to the accompaniment of the *Ogumh*, the Igede *sanza*. The rotating part-harmony of these songs shows traces of an archaic hocketing style that is less evident in more modern Igede music. Some of these songs are in obscure dialects whose meaning has been forgotten. In Igede, the use of the *ogumh* tends to be reserved for the recreation of the elderly, although playing it can be a source of income for disabled people who have no other means of livelihood. While living among the Igede, I recorded the songs and tunes of Okpo Ikogi, a masquerade costume weaver and elder. He described himself not as a singer, but as a proverb reciter. He used the *ogumh* as a talking instrument, which repeated his spoken Igede greeting. This use of the thumb piano is unusual.[11]

As in most cultures, the Igede have various lullabies that mothers and other adult females sing to sooth or entertain babies and small children. Some of these songs involve physical movement, where the child is rocked or patted. One popular game mothers and infants play entails the mother tossing the child into the air as she sings *"Apwu Ejii pwu ka gbaji ka uhe"* ("You Can't Yet Reach Yet You're Jumping Up")[12] Thus, a formative link between music and movement is established early in the child's life.

For Igede children, drumming and dancing are a major form of play. More of their playtime is spent with these activities than any other form of recreation. As youngsters of any society, whose play involves the imitation of adult activities, Igede children meticulously observe the required form. The all-male adult musical groups have their infant counterparts, where children arrange themselves around three tin-can drums, which substitute for the adult groups's *ubah*, *egbong*, and *okpirih*.

Although young adolescent girls are the main proponents, children of both sexes enjoy dancing the current traditional dances, such as the *Ogbete* circle dance. They also sing and clap to Igede hymns they learn in bible class. Unhindered by the lack of appropriate costumes, the children are always ready to improvise. Mango leaves, for example, may be threaded around their ankles to represent leg rattles. I, myself, observed an infant boy don a polyethylene headdress in imitation of the masquerade.

Igede adults encourage musical activity among the children. Happy to see musical traditions perpetuated, they are glad also that the young are learning skills that will supply the future society with accomplished musicians. As a result, by the time the Igede child is about seven years old, he or she has developed a high level of rhythmic sophistication and dance ability.

Music of the Peer Group

Traditionally, age-grade organizations were very much a feature of Igede life. These were manifested in the three levels of "secret" society, secret in the sense that members were not supposed to discuss their activities with nonmembers. Additionally nonmembers were forbidden to see members in session. The first initiation for boys was into the *Ogorigo* society; the members of *Ogorigo*, in turn, expected to graduate into the *Ukpe* society when they reached adolescence. The highest level of initiation for male adults was *Achuku*, the principal sociopolitical decision-making body in Igede.

Ogorigo and *Ukpe* societies served a number of useful functions. They were considered necessary preparation for *Achuku*, thus a training ground for future leadership. They were socializing agencies, assisting in the development of stable individuals, who would be socially responsible and democratically attuned. They fostered a team spirit and a disciplined approach to life, which facilitated the development of shared interests and friendship among the agemates of a village.

Today, *Achuku* is still very much a part of Igede life and is likely to remain so. But with many youth receiving their secondary education in boarding schools beyond Igede territory, the *Ogorigo* and *Ukpe* societies appear to be on the decline. Church organizations, student associations, and other youth groups have replaced them to some extent.

Nevertheless, the musical functions of the younger age-grades are still very much in evidence. To insure that the musical traditions of the community are perpetuated, each village encourages its young people to form a childrens' dance guild. The youngest member is about five years old, while the upper limit may be stretched to include a few sixteen-year-olds to round out the harmony by contributing voices in a lower register.

The structure of these peer group associations parallels that of the adult group. Like the adult music association, they operate under the patronage of an influential and respected adult leader, who becomes their *Ada-ilo* (father of play). The associations also feature managing functionaries, such as an *Akiraa* (secretary) and *Alijwoh* (directors), who play a vital role in organizing the group and arranging public performances.

The two youth groups I documented, the *Omepa* of Oju, and the *Onyeweh* of Andibla, both featured masquerades from whom they derived their name (see figures 7.5 and 7.6). These youthful masquerades were awarded the same respect as their adult counterparts. Before the masquerades appeared, sanctified water was sprinkled over the dance arena to disperse evil spirits, just as for adult masquerades. Youth groups employ the same triad of drums as the adult group, sometimes supplemented by basketwork rattles and a whistle. The whistle is primarily used by youth groups and is an essential ingredient of such dances as *Iboma, Imeri,* and *Ogbete.* Certain prestigious instruments—such as the signal instruments, the *ogirigboh* (slit-gong) and *opikeh* (antelope horn), or the emblematic *iyachi* (iron spear with clappers) and the calabash horns of the Ogirinye warrior association—are reserved for adult use.

Girls, although not excluded from the male associations, usually prefer to form *Ogbete* guilds or to play traditional dancing games, such as *Oge.* Unlike the youthful masquerade associations, which mirror the adult guilds and function as training grounds for adult performers of the future, *Ogbete, Imeri,* and *Oge* associations are strictly the province of children and young adolescents.

Figure 7.5 The *Omepa* children's musical association of Obohu village, Oju (R. Nicholls)

Figure 7.6 The *Onyeweh* children's masquerades of Andibla (R. Nicholls)

In a community where children traditionally spend long hours working alongside the adults, time away from the compound for recreation is a necessity. On moonlit evenings, boys and girls steal away to the meeting ground to play those universal games such as tag or to dance such dances as *Ogbete* or *Oge*. *Ogbete*[13] bears witness to the continuity of tradition. As the successor to *Imeri*, it is a relatively modern dance, which originated around 1960. It is danced vigorously in a circle by unmarried adolescents of both sexes around a single male drummer. The dancers sing as they dance and, as an adolescent counterpart of *Imwo*, the adult women's association, the group expresses social criticism through song, and the lyrics are usually satirical. In the *Oge* dance, two lines face each other. The dancers perform intricate steps and engage in a teasing repartee, calling for a response from each participant in turn. Thus, *Oge* both polishes physical coordination and sharpens the wits.

It should be noted that while adults encourage children to develop skill in music and dance, the children receive no overt training from them. From my observation, it seems that the children learn primarily through imitation, imitating both adult musicians and the more talented members of the peer group. A clearly developed sense of good performance permeates the peer group associations and careless musicianship is not tolerated.

In the past, an institution known as *Adiya* (dance queen) existed, in which formal dance training was awarded the personable young girls who possessed the required degree of talent. These girls were elected in pairs, one dark in complexion (*omilonya*) and the other fair (*aloho*). During the five to seven years of their training, they would live in the compound of *Adiya*, situated at some distance from the village. This was to avoid the distracting attentions of would-be suitors. The *Adiya* performance was preceded by the dances of the attendant maids. The *Adiya* dancers were carried to the arena on a mat, as their feet were not supposed to touch ordinary ground. *Adiya* is now virtually extinct.[14]

Music in the Church

The impact of Christianity and Western values seems to have adversely affected female dance traditions in Igede. In one way, the church can be viewed as a liberating factor, for it has brought the Igede women out of the compound and involved them in local activities which are under the auspices of the church. This has led, however, to a decline in female involvement in dance as well as in other traditional activities (*Adiya* fulfilled a specific function within the New Yam Festival, probably in the role of a fertility symbol). Some Igede hymns actively condemn traditional religious observances. One chorus ("Anyi nyohe a'kpojiga ka") contains the instruction "Children of God don't *make devotions to traditional gods.*"[15]

Status conscious parishioners tend not to consider dance as a serious activity for adult women. One young lady, a member of a teachers' college choir, explained to me that she joined the choir when she felt she was too old for her *Ogbete* dance association.[16] Igede hymns are typically lively and may be accompanied by the *ota-ubah* (an aerophonic pot-drum introduced into Igede by Ibo missionaries), metal maracas, and hand-clapping. The vigorous participation in the hymn singing probably serves as a partial substitute for the dance. Drums and other traditional instruments are not allowed in Igede churches, with the exception of the few branches of the Yoruba-originated Cherubim and Seraphin church that have recently become established in some areas of Igede.

The Igede church congregation is predominantly female. Men may combine participation in church music with membership in a music association, but a distinction is made between the two. Igede hymns, lively though they may be, remain simply *songs* to the Igede and do not satisfy the need for creative performance contained in Igede dance traditions. Among the surviving female music traditions, *Imwo* songs continue, and I documented a performance by the *Abwo* (Bamboo) womens' dance guild of Andibla. The *Abwo* association members adopt a crescent-shaped formation around solo-dances performed by fellow members. They are named after the bamboo clapping-sticks that they use to accompany the songs.

Many myths and generalizations have been generated about Africa, and some of them are concerned with music and dance. Music and dance is often depicted as being an ever-present part of daily activities arising spontaneously whenever the need is felt. My experience in Oju L.G.A. emphasizes the fact that music and dance is

a highly regarded element of traditional life and there is nothing haphazard or impromptu about music or dance occasions.

Igede music and dance reaches the height of its presentation
during funerals and is a means by which man is in contact with the
ancestral world. In this contact a high degree of form is observed
which is established by tradition; thus, very little is left to chance.
By exploring the intrinsic link between aesthetics and ideology that
is embodied in the Igede funeral ceremony, a study of music guilds
in Igede gives an insight into the role the arts play in making an
ideology more salient on ritual occasions. In common with many of
the oral traditions of Africa, Igede religious beliefs are not simply
theoretical or contemplative in nature but live within the activities
by which they are expressed. In such societies a ritual becomes the
medium by which the principles, values, and qualities thought
crucial to the welfare of the community are expressed. Modern educational thought reminds us that values are not learned by "learning about" something, but by going through experiences which
touch the feelings, thereby affecting the core of the personality.
(Taba: 1962) Fundamental values relating to kinship, the ancestors,
tradition, and the Igede perception of life and death, are contained
within the funeral ceremony. The need for a formalized relation
with the ancestors permeates Igede musical activities and has been
responsible for the formation of musical associations, which in turn
are highly structured.

NOTES

1. The figure is a projection based on the 1963 national census which
then reported the population of Igede as 160,616.

2. Whilst in Igede I recorded a variety of traditional music, including
warrior associations, social music types, children's songs, and church
music. Ranung's (1973) long-playing record *Music of Dawn and Day* is the
only album of Igede music available commercially. A comparison of music
styles in the northwest of Herskovits' "Congo Area" can be obtained by
contrasting Igede music to the music of the Beti, Bamileke, and Bamoun
ethnic groups in Cameroon. This latter music is available on the Radiodiffusion Televison Francaise (1963) album *Musique du Cameroun*. Bjorn
Ranung, a Swedish anthropologist, made his recordings of Igede music
between September 1971 and February 1972. On his liner notes, which give
an account of Igede music guilds, he has noted that the "Igede are a people

very little known in anthropological literature. They are mentioned among the Southern Nigerians in G. P. Murdock's survey of the peoples of Africa, and they are given a few pages in R. G. Armstrong's monograph on the Idoma-speaking peoples in the Ethnographic Survey of Africa published by the International African Institute."

3. For an example of what Chapman and Turnbull (1961) describe as the "hocketing" or "durchbroken Arbeit" technique listen to *Music of the Ituri Forest*.

4. A mask of the Oju *Aitah* masquerade depicts a little man cutting off the head of a snake. Possibly the snake symbolizes the foe and the man is a warrior, in the act of collecting a trophy head. A fuller discussion of the practice of taking trophy heads can be found in Kasfir (1985), Nicholls (1984), and Nicklin (1974 & 1979).

5. Ochi Ekoma, personal communication, 1978.

6. Sachs (1963: 74) writes that abstract or "imageless" funeral dances in the form of a circle are performed in a number of "planter cultures." The idea behind them is to form a tie between the living and the dead by means of ecstatic dance and to make it possible for the soul of the deceased to find his ancestors.

7. An interesting parallel associating the ancestors with the dawn comes from the other end of the African continent, among the Zulu. An informant from the Mamelodi Township of Pretoria tells of the practice of *ukuphahla*, a form of private thanksgiving to the ancestors, performed before the night's sleep. During *ukuphahla* the individual kneels facing the east, where the sun rises. As with the Igede, the ancestors are associated with the dawn. Sunrise symbolizes "good things, a new day and new hopes." Keletso Denalane, personal communication, 1984.

8. For information on the Igede funeral see Idikwu (1976).

9. A discussion of dance as a form of nonverbal communication is provided by Hanna (1980).

10. Mark Alagi, personal communication, 1978.

11. Dr. Ken Gourlay the ethnomusicologist, informed me that this was the first time he had come across the use of the *sanza* as a talking instrument. Personal communication, 1979.

12. Grace Ode, personal communication, 1979.

13. *Ogbete* is the name of a sweet alcoholic wine made from guinea corn.

14. J. O. Ochelle, personal communication, 1978.

15. The Igede word *"kpojiga"* is a composite term representing a range of observances made to traditional gods, including *okpukpu* (animal sacrifice) and the putting of food at the base of the *Ohe-Ogbadogogo Ubwo* tree.

16. Oto'o Obaike, personal communication, 1978.

REFERENCES

Anon. 1980. *This Is Oju LGA* (Local Government Area). Prepared and published by Directorate of Information Governor's Office, Makurdi. Kaduna, Nigeria: Sooji Press.

Chapman, Francis S., and Turnbull, Colin M. 1961. *Music of the Ituri Forest*. Long playing record album. New York: Ethnic Folkways Library.

Gourlay, K. A. 1979. "Towards the Differentiation of Music Areas in Nigeria Through the Distribution of Musical Instruments," Seminar paper, June 6, 1979, Center for Nigerian Cultural Studies, Ahmadu Bello Univesity, Zaria, Nigeria.

Hanna, Judith Lynne. 1980. *To Dance Is Human: A Theory of Nonverbal Communication*. Austin: University of Texas Press.

Herskovits, Melville J. 1948. *Man and His Works: The Source of Cultural Anthropology*. New York: Borzoi Books, Alfred A. Knopf, Inc.

Idikiwu, Simon Eriba. 1976. *Burial in Igede*. Self-published booklet. Oju L.G.A., Nigeria.

Kasfir, Sidney L. 1985. "Celebrating Male Aggression: The Idoma Oglinye Masquerade." In *Tricksters, Transvestites and Warriors: African Masks and Cultural Systems*, ed. S. L. Kasfir.

Middleton, J. 1960. *Lugbara Religion*. New York: Oxford University Press.

Nicholls, R. W. 1984. "Igede Funeral Masquerades," *African Arts* Vol. 17, No. 3, pp. 70-76, Los Angeles: University of California at Los Angeles.

Nicklin, Keith. 1974. "Nigerian Skin Covered Masks," *African Arts* Vol. 7, No. 3, Los Angeles: University of California at Los Angeles.

_____. 1979. "Skin-Covered Masks of Cameroon," *African Arts* Vol. 12, No. 2, Los Angeles: University of California at Los Angeles.

Okita, S.I.O. 1973. "The Historical Evolution of Religious and Related Ideas and Practices in Igede." B.A. dissertation, history, Ahmadu Bello University, Zaria, Nigeria.

Radiodiffusion Television Francaise. 1963. *Musique du Cameroun*. Long playing record album. Paris: Office du Radiodiffusion Televison Francaise.

Ranung, Bjorn. 1973. *Music of Dawn and Day*. Long playing record album. Finland: Love Records.

Sachs, Curt. 1963. *World History of the Dance*. New York: W. W. Morton & Co.

Taba, Hilda. 1962. *Curriculum Development: Theory and Practice*. New York: Harcourt, Brace & World.

Ecstatic Singing: Music and Social Integration in an African Church

The African Apostolic Church is a syncretic religious sect that was founded in 1932 by John Maranke, a self-styled Shona visionary. Over the past two decades, the African Apostles have spread rapidly from their base in eastern Zimbabwe to five Central African nations. The group's autonomous congregations are politically linked to the original church center near Umtali in eastern Zimbabwe. Elsewhere (1975a: 187-214), I have analyzed the history and complex ceremonial format of Apostolic worship. Here, I will focus on music as a source of social integration in Apostolic rituals.[1]

Ecstatic singing is an important component of all Apostolic worship ceremonies. As sect members sing, they enter a trance state. At this time, they believe they witness a spiritual presence. This, in turn, demonstrates their intense personal involvement in worship. For the Apostles, music cannot be separated from the ritual contexts in which it is performed. Therefore, an overview of singing in Apostolic ceremonies first requires an explanation of the beliefs and practices of the group.

THE STRUCTURE OF APOSTOLIC CEREMONIES

Like many indigenous African sects, the Apostles combine Judeo-Christian doctrines with traditional African customs (cf. Barrett 1968: 154-158). They replace beliefs in ancestral and alien spirits with faith in the intervention of the Holy Spirit. The Apostles believe that a religious utopia is spiritually recreated with each formal act of worship.

Following Old Testament directives, the Apostles conduct their worship ceremonies on Saturdays. The *kerek* or weekly Sabbath ceremony, held outdoors, is the major Apostolic worship event.[2] This particular ceremony symbolically represents the descent of the Holy Spirit and the angels into the place of prayer or the "New Jerusalem." During the ceremony, the Apostles enact a day of judgment in which the "sinners" are symbolically separated from the "saved" souls. Singing is a critical element in sustaining the group's sense of collective religious identity as a chosen spiritual elite.

Whenever a group of Apostles meets to pray and sing, a state of worship is invoked by calling, *"kerek! kerek! kerek!"* Thus, *kerek* refers to both a full ceremony and the spiritual state of participants in prayer.

There are three types of singing in Apostolic ceremonies: formal hymns, didactic songs, and ecstatic chants. These song formats may be placed on a continuum of emotional intensity. The same "song" may be relegated to more than one category, depending on the stage in the ceremony when it is performed. All opening and closing hymns are sung in Chishona, the ritual language of the original Zimbabwean Apostles (see appendix). It is believed that the Shona language is the appropriate format for communication between man and God, even for members who do not speak that language fluently.

In regional congregations, other African vernaculars are used for the didactic songs and ecstatic chants. During the course of a single ceremony, Apostles generally sing in three to five distinctive African dialects. Furthermore, glossolalia is introduced into ecstatic singing as a way of demonstrating that the worshippers have direct contact with the angels and the Holy Spirit. These glossolalic utterances, which may also be classified into several subcategories —ranging from ritual formulas to unintelligible vocalizations— occur in both Apostolic sermons and Apostolic songs, once an ecstatic peak of worship is reached.

Apostolic singing is, thus, linguistically diverse. New songs are translated into several languages for each congregation. Nevertheless, they retain distinctive harmonic patterns, and song leaders always use a complex call-response format. A similar responsorial format is characteristic of Apostolic preaching. It stimulates the group's participation in each part of the ceremony.

Two opening hymns are sung in Chishona to call the angels into the place of prayer: *"Kwese, Kwese"* ("Everywhere, Everywhere"), adapted from the Chishona Methodist hymnal, and *"Mwari Komborera Africa"* ("God Save Africa").[3] "God Save Africa" is commonly used by many indigenous churches and is an anthem for political groups throughout southern Africa. The emphasis in political renditions, however, is on God and the land of Africa, rather than on the Holy Spirit and Jesus as in the Apostolic version.[4] The Apostolic refrain, for example, is:

> O Come Spirit,
> Come Holy Spirit,
> Bless us.
> O Holy Spirit, God, Father,
> Jesus,
> Bless us!*

This invocation may be compared to customary Chishona songs that are used to summon ancestral spirits for worship.

The act of singing is believed to produce the Holy Spirit's immediate presence. This particular hymn is performed slowly and solemnly, with little variation from one congregation to another. In *"Mwari Komborera Africa,"* Jesus is perceived as part of the Holy Trinity. This is noteworthy because of the so-called weak Christology of the Apostles (Murphree 1969: 101). The Apostles consider themselves to be Christians and do not substitute a black Messiah for Christ. John Maranke, the prophet-founder, is viewed as a messenger to the people of Africa. He, according to Apostolic followers, reinterpreted the scriptures for the African continent. Depending on the worship context, Jesus is regarded as a figure in the Holy Trinity, a prophet, a healer, an angel, or a spiritual ancestor. When the name of Jesus is invoked in the *"Mwari,"* it signifies His presence amidst the congregation and affirms the members' readiness to worship.

A closing hymn (*"Ndo Famba"*), meaning "Our Worship Has Ended," is sung in Chishona at the end of the *kerek* ceremony. The

---

*NOTE: Texts throughout are author's translations from fieldwork.

Apostles believe that the angels depart at this point, returning when the next occasion for worship arises. All songs initiated between the opening and the closing portions of *kerek* are voluntary and, to a certain extent, spontaneous. As the ceremony continues, the worshippers reach an ecstatic peak and chanting begins.

CEREMONIAL PROCEDURES FOR INITIATING SONGS

Song initiation among the Apostles takes a form common to many indigenous churches: the songs are not written down and the texts are highly improvisational. Basic and free-floating verses are taught in song sessions that occur outside the formal ceremony. In the *kerek*, singing is interspersed with preaching. Once the opening hymns have been performed, church members interrupt freely with didactic songs. Apostles consider these songs to be a form of preaching because they interpret specific biblical texts and provide members with moral directives for their daily conduct. While the time when songs appear is not governed by a desire for overall unity within the service and no set number of songs is performed, there is an expectation that certain songs will emphasize and heighten the moral content of sermons. In most Sabbath ceremonies, there are at least three preachers who work closely with Bible readers of their choice. The managing evangelist (or ceremonial manager) for the *kerek* selects the preachers beforehand and advises them about appropriate biblical passages.

Women are seated to the west and men to the east of the congregational grounds. This arrangement facilitates the intercession of separate men's and women's singing groups. Much of the preaching that I witnessed was both spatially and verbally directed toward the women's side of the congregation. Preachers also aim comments at particular subgroups of elders.[5] Women are exhorted not to engage in extravagances and to be obedient wives. The men, in turn, are encouraged to follow the teachings of the church strictly and to provide for the family and community. When selectively focusing their preaching in this way, they anticipate an antiphonal spoken or musical response from the subgroup.

Pauses in the sermon sequence mark appropriate points for congregational singing. Apostles explain that the congregation should never be silent during worship, for the sound of the people's voices in prayer and song is a message to God. Thus, although singing is not mandatory at each pause, it is tacitly expected as a means of filling gaps in the sermon presentations.

These expectable moments for singing constitute the ceremonial backdrop for musical improvisation. When the preacher stops to announce to the collaborating reader his topic and biblical passages, there is a pause. The first song is then usually initiated by a song leader or, less frequently, by the presiding preacher. The introduction of subsequent passages produces additional pauses during which time it is appropriate for the worshippers to sing. These pauses create a "coherence factor" in singing. That is, the congregation is primed to sing at speaker-reader pauses throughout the ceremony.

At the outset, the content of these songs is didactic. Song leaders elaborate upon the biblical passages and messages the speakers present. In their interactions with the congregation, these song leaders use "overlapped antiphony" (cf. Lomax 1970: 193), rather than a simple call-response pattern. As a result, the choral response overlaps with the opening verse that the song leader recites. The following excerpt illustrates the explicit character of the singers' elaborations on biblical texts:

Speaker: I thank God the Creator for the multitudes of people. I thank
Jehovah of Israel because he puts me before you to bring you his
will. I am really a prophet and the work of any prophet is for
the goodness of the children of Israel. He cares for them. But as I
stand here, I see the crowd, I see them like thirsty flocks without
a shepherd. . . .

Song leader (initiates didactic song):

Verse: It is time to sing for our Lord.
It is time to sing for Jerusalem.
We sing and ask for grace.

Refrain: Come to song and the sound
Of the drum of Life.
Everybody read Hoseah verse
four at 11.
Cigarette smoking and alcohol
detain you from God.
Come out of houses made of mud,
We sing and ask mercy of God.
Our main preoccupation
now is to sing!

The last two lines of the refrain emphasize the emotional shift that occurs in the congregation once song has been initiated. Not only does the first song forecast the didactic message of the sermon, it also stresses that the congregation has a duty to witness this message and give praise through song. When this type of song takes hold, it may escalate to a chant through the repetition of the refrain and the dropping of verses. The refrain may eventually be reduced to the chanting of a few key phrases. Since new verses may be improvised or repeated without a fixed termination point, the preacher must be forceful enough to redirect the congregation's attention to the sermon. The ritualized greeting "Life to you Apostles, Peace be with you!" is one means of arresting a song. The speaker shouts this greeting until he regains the congregation's attention and can resume the sermon. If the song dies out on its own, this greeting also enlivens the ceremony and provides a smooth transition back to the sermon.

The prophet who resumed preaching following the above excerpt did so by shouting the ritualized greeting and then qualifying it: "Looking at how we sing, it is not necessary that I preach the gospel now. I preach the gospel only because I feel sorry for your souls. . . ." This statement establishes the importance of preaching in relationship to didactic songs. Preaching the gospel is considered a means to educate the congregation and any outsiders who may be attending the ceremony. Singing reinforces the emotional content of each message, but Apostles assert that outsiders cannot easily understand the religious meaning of their songs.

In addition, congregational singing is an avenue for counteracting the speaker's message. Singers are explicit about the political conflicts within the congregation and freely express their views of the church leaders' moral and spiritual standings. When several Zairean Apostolic congregations experienced a political rift in the early 1970s, a popular song intoned, "We want Musumbu [a prominent Zairean church elder] and not Nawezi as our leader." Although such explicitly divisive songs are discouraged by the church center, they continue to be improvised as a way of dramatizing current events.[6]

Much more common, however, are songs initiated by women or by younger men as warnings or counter-sermons to the church elders. Women in the church may hold the spiritual ranks of healers (*barapi*) and prophetesses (*baprofiti*). As such, women are formally forbidden from preaching before the congregation. They may, nevertheless, hold the position of special singers ("High Cross" or *maharikros*) along with the men. Whether they are publicly recognized as special singers or not, it is expected that women will interrupt sermons with songs. This type of song interruption is a ceremonial prerogative for women. Thus, they cannot be censured for the critical content of didactic songs.

One song that is popular among women in a Zambian congregation has the following refrain: "Men, stop beating your wives. Only then will you go to heaven." This song was often interjected as a warning to presiding preachers and other male elders. This critical license to express rebellious sentiments and poignant moral criticisms through song often results in a verbal "tug of war" between the male elders and the women song leaders. Since regaining the floor after a pause is problematic for speakers, when women initiate songs, they are able to compete for control of the service. If they succeed in achieving enough momentum through particularly lively singing or ecstatic chanting, they override the sermon. In my observations over several years of research, however, such occasions were indeed rare.

It is noteworthy that while the process of song initiation brings congregational conflicts into the open, the end result is generally unifying. Incipient conflicts are momentarily resolved through singing and thus the moral integration of the group is strengthened.

THE RELATIONSHIP BETWEEN PREACHERS AND WOMEN SONG LEADERS

The continual shifting between sermons and song sustains a rhythmic alternation of activities throughout the *kerek*. This balance represents the ideal equilibrium between male and female members of the group. Apostles contend that women are the *spiritual* equals of men. Thus, they are encouraged to express themselves through ceremonial, although not political, leadership. As already stated, the preacher's limited control of the ceremony relies on his ability to regain the floor following a lively or prolonged song. Often women initiate songs as a group. In one congregation, the women singers rehearsed before the *kerek* and initiated the lead vocal lines in unison. The rest of the congregation then followed them. As a result, the women were able to control the intensity and duration of the singing and to convey their verbal message before being interrupted by the preacher.

In many cases, however, the equilibrium between male and female participation collapses. If a lone women tentatively initiates a song without the support of other women, the verse may be transferred to a male lead singer. On the conclusion of the female's first lead, a man simply initiates the next verse, often in a falsetto voice. If a woman's didactic messages make the rest of the congregation uncomfortable, a managing evangelist stops the song with a ceremonial greeting in order to allow the speaker to finish. This happens, too, when several songs are performed in succession, whether they are initiated by male or female song leaders. Thus, ecstatic singing may be terminated by the ceremonial manager, who returns the floor to the preacher. The desired balance between preaching the gospel and singing hymns of praise, alluded to in our previous excerpt, is maintained through this technique.

Women are instrumental in the improvisation process. They develop new songs and variations on old tunes. They rehearse these songs in their worship groups outside of *kerek*. Cooperation among women is critical to the introduction of new variations. If the subgroup carries off the variations, the entire congregation eventually accepts the new verses and they spread to other congregations. The daughter of a leading elder in the Lusaka congregation originated several songs in this manner.

THE CONTENT OF APOSTOLIC SONGS

Apostolic group singing is polyphonic. All rhythmic and harmonic gaps are filled. Consequently, it is difficult for the Western listener to locate the melody and musical themes of Apostolic songs (cf. Jones 1959: 224-227).[7] Women initiate song innovations by shifting the harmonic patterns, making only minimal changes in words. Men modify the melody by singing falsetto imitations of women's voices and thus change verse innovations. In this way, singing becomes an arena for both competition and subgroup cooperation.

Whether they are sung by men or women, Apostolic songs are open-ended. Certain song texts are used as free-floating verses that can be inserted into other tunes (see figure 8.1). Textual variations also produce slight changes in tunes. A song's total configuration consists of the modifications across its performances in different contexts. There are many possibilities for such variation. Figures 8.1 and 8.2 (Jules-Rosette 1975c: 160) present two tunes, commonly sung with extensive variations and free-floating verse additions. "Sodom and Gomorrah" (figure 8.2) was sung with different verses and tune variations on each occasion that I heard it.[8] The basic text (figure 8.2) is used as a point of departure for these innovations.

Figure 8.1 *Variations in tunes*: "I put my heart in God"

Figure 8.2 *Variations in tunes*: "Earth is Sodom and Gomorrah"

Although the performances of "I Put My Heart in God" (figure 8.1) varied less, it followed the same pattern. Since drums, rattles, and other instrumentation are forbidden by the Apostles (cf. Chernoff 1979: 100-102), rhythmic modifications are created by *ngoma*, a technique in which singers yodel and muffle their voices to imitate the sound of trumpets and drums.[9] Although *ngoma* are generally initiated by men, both men and women provide this accompaniment during the chorus.

THE DIDACTIC CONTENT OF CEREMONIAL SONGS

Apostles make clear distinctions between hymns, songs of praise, and calls to obey the church and moral laws. The latter two are didactic in nature. They are intended to teach the congregation about its moral and spiritual obligations. While songs of praise express thanks to the Holy Spirit for the congregation's state of worship, they also urge members to rejoice in the teachings of the church. Consider, for example, this song of praise:

"WE HAVE GATHERED"
(TSHILUBA, ADAPTED FROM
CHISHONA, "*TAUNGANE TENZI*")

Tshiluba	English
Taunga, taunga, taungane, Mambo wa ku denga	We have gathered, we have gathered, Lord in Heaven
Tuimbayi, tuimbayi, taungane,	Let us sing, we have gathered
Mambo wa ku denga	Lord in Heaven
Tuakengi, tuakengi, etc.	Let us learn, we have gathered
Osana, tuakengi, etc.	Lord in Heaven Hosanna, let us learn, etc.
Balunda, tuimbayi, etc.	Friends, let us sing, etc.
Baprofiti, imbayi, etc.	Prophets, sing, etc.
Bavengeri, imbayi, etc.	Evangelists, sing, etc.
Bamama, imbayi, etc.	Women, sing, etc.
Bapostolo, imbayi, etc.	Apostles, sing, etc.
Yezu katshia waya, etc.	Since Jesus departed, etc.

This song encourages members of all ranks within the church to engage in collective praise singing. The repeated verses are relatively simple. Therefore, "*Taungane*" easily lends itself to chanting, as the verses fall off and worshippers repeat the vocal theme several times. This song is often used to enliven a sermon and to escalate the ceremony into ecstatic singing. John Maranke (1953: 12) records that his brothers, Cornelius and Anrod, performed this song joyously on the day (July 17, 1932) that he first received the message to preach publicly and found the church.

Apostles believe that they face temptation constantly once they have been baptized. Consequently, there are songs that exhort members to keep the laws of the church and remind them that the task is difficult. For example:

"THE BAPTISM OF JOHN"
(ORIGINALLY IN TSHILUBA,
"*DIBATIZA DIA YONA*")

Tshiluba	English
Dibatiza dia Yona ndia bualu bukole	The baptism of John is difficult
Satana muimana Yesu muimana belangana mpata	Satan stands here, Jesus there, they are fighting
Buloba bujima butukonka bua Nyuma wa Nzambi	The whole earth asks us about the Holy Spirit
Mikenji kayena mu diulu, kayena dishiya dia mayi	The laws are not in Heaven nor on the other bank of the river
Mikenji bakayifunda mu Mukanda wa Nzambi	The laws are written in the Bible
Wayenza ne wayilama neasungidibue	He who does and keeps them will be saved
Mambo wa Mambo, midimu ya kubuikila buloba bujima we	Lord God, the darkness was spread out over the whole earth
Munya wakatemena bakamuibabeya, O Baba	Light was revealed to those who believed, O Father
Bakadia mubidi ne mashi bia mfumuetu Yesu	Those who ate the body and blood of our Lord Jesus

The baptism of John refers to the Holy Spirit baptism that initiates Apostles into the group. The allusion to the baptism of John creates a biblical *double entendre* in the song. The reference is both to the biblical account of Jesus' baptism by John in the wilderness and to the baptism of the Apostles of John Maranke. The implication is that both baptisms are accompanied by weighty religious obligations. Hence, the Apostles reason that it was difficult for Jesus to live up to his baptism, and they anticipate similar temptations for their members.

Songs of praise urge members to rejoice in the teachings of the church while the calls to obey the law remind them of the obligations that they must uphold.[10] Within both songs and sermons, the terms that refer to members and outsiders shift accordingly. When they rejoice in their chosen path, Apostles refer to themselves as "we." "You" references in songs and sermons designate members in need of correction or encouragement. The pronoun "they" addresses outsiders who have, thus far, refused to accept the Apostolic way. Through switching these terms of reference in song verses, Apostles develop a sense of moral community.

SINGING AS AN EXPRESSION OF MORAL COMMUNITY

Moral community is expressed by pointing to those who wish to follow the laws of the church as a source of spiritual improvement. For Apostles, singing is a microcosm of intragroup relationships. The "we" verses express the collective spiritual aims of the group. One verse of "I Put my Heart in God" asserts:

> I put my heart in God.
> *We* are passengers, *we* are passengers.
> *We* are not baptized from the cup.
> *We* are sons of Heaven.

When Apostles refer to themselves as "we," they also designate their readiness for spiritual salvation.

The "you" verses found in many didactic songs dramatize the spiritual struggle of the Apostles:

> *You* who wish to pray, pray from this moment on
> *You* who are taught how to sing, *you* will inherit Heaven

You who are asleep, get up, *you* will miss Heaven
You who are staying because of drinking, *you* will miss Heaven
God is good to worship so *you* go to Heaven

"They" verses single out individuals who turn away from God's message. These outsiders have been exposed to moral exhortations, but thus far to no avail. The following didactic verse exemplifies this process:

We told them, Lord; *they* refused
The people have eyes; *they* have no ears
The people look but *they* do not see
They refuse Jesus, the Jews
Light shone on those who believed
Those who walk in light shall judge the world

In closing verses, for example, "Our main preoccupation is to sing," Apostles identify themselves as a collectivity of singers.

One rendition of "Sodom and Gomorrah" contains the following closing verses:

Please sing out all your sins
It is time to sing for our Lord
It is time to sing for Jesus
We sing and ask for grace
Today's throne is to sing

These "we" verses differ from routine didactic exhortations. They emphasize that the Apostles are building a sense of collective unity through the act of singing. As they sing together, Apostles believe that they are creating an image of themselves as saints who are prepared to enter the heavenly city. When this state of cohesiveness has been reached, Apostles strive to imitate their conception of angels' voices. These song-chants represent the peak of Apostolic worship. (See figures 8.3 and 8.4.)

SINGING AS AN ECSTATIC STATE

Through ecstatic singing, Apostles learn to channel their emotions and express their religious sentiments publicly. They

Figure 8.3 Apostolic women concentrate intensely as they sing the closing hymn at *kerek*, Lusaka, Zambia

Figure 8.4 *Maharikros* (special singers) in Bocha, Zimbabwe perform a praise song after the worship ceremony

enter a state of *collective* trance during which they witness the presence of both the Holy Spirit and the angels. At this point, other social preoccupations recede. This state differs from the self-induced trance (cf. Walker 1972: 25-50), which may occur at any point during the *kerek* Sabbath ceremony. Communal trance, while achieved as the song leader progressively drops the verses from a song and repeats single phrases or words, is never credited to a particular individual.

As the verses fall away during ecstatic singing, standard phrases such as "God in Heaven" ("*Mambo wa ku denga*") or "Maranke in Heaven" ("*Maranke wa ku denga*") are repeated. These phrases reinforce the sense of spiritual communion within the congregation. During chanting, the rhythmic shape of the song is transformed as worshippers put increasing emphasis on strongly accented beats. The effect resembles the intensification of drumming in customary African trance-dance performances (cf. Chernoff 1979: 111-112). While the rhythm is accentuated, the harmonies of the chorus tighten. The loose collection of voices described as a part of didactic singing becomes a tight, single unit. The overall effect is hypnotic. The rhythmic and harmonic modifications push the singers into a state of maximum spiritual involvement. As the chant proceeds, individuals moan, yodel, and insert *ngoma* (percussive vocalizations) and glossolalic utterances. The entire congregation sways to the rhythm, but dancing per se is disallowed as is the use of musical instruments.

Ecstatic singing separates the group insiders (or "the saved") from outsiders. It is believed that outsiders who have not confessed and received an Apostolic baptism cannot reach the ecstatic peaks of song-trance attained by true members. Still the harmonies and rhythms of Apostolic chanting, embellished with glossolalic shouts, are so distinctive that outsiders recognize and attempt to imitate them. At a rare joint ceremony held between the Maranke Apostles and a closely related group, the Apostles of John Masowe, the guests shared in preaching and song with their hosts.[11] When ecstatic singing began, the outsiders intoned "Je-hovah!" and spoke in tongues. After the ceremony, Maranke members criticized the undisciplined singing and participation of their guests as insincere, but they admitted that some of the Masowe members could sing well. In other words, Masowe members were able to follow the cadence and rhythm of ecstatic singing, even though their hosts did not acknowledge the validity of their spiritual experience. The Maranke songs were used to maintain boundaries between the groups. Yet group singing also fostered a sense of ecumenical unity.

For Apostles, ecstatic singing must be undertaken with a "pure heart" because it is witnessed by God and the angels. Cries of "Amen!" "Jesus!" and glossolalic utterances attest to this spiritual presence. Sustaining chants over a long period of time is considered evidence of the congregation's correct moral standing. Similar chants employed during curing sessions are believed to insure the success of faith healing.

Ecstatic songs in *kerek* are also viewed as a form of meditation. Through singing, members derive strength to face the problems and temptations of the outside world. Ecstatic singing is the most highly valued phase of group worship.[12]

MUSIC AS A SOURCE OF SOCIAL INTEGRATION AMONG THE APOSTLES

For Apostles, didactic singing defines and strengthens community ideals. Through didactic songs, elders instruct new members about church standards and exhort older members to follow the Apostolic way. As the case of women song leaders illustrates, didactic singing is also an arena for expressing and resolving intragroup conflicts. Timely songs about recent events dramatize the emergence of new leaders and political factions. Rank-and-file men and women air their grievances through song. Latent conflicts that would eventually disrupt the community are also aired.[13]

Despite the fact that speakers and singers vie for control of the worship service, ecstatic chanting establishes social integration and a sense of equilibrium. It also provides a major source of catharsis.[14] During song-trance, group competition disappears and a state of spiritual peace becomes the communal goal. A shared musical and social harmony overrides conflicts (Schutz 1964: 159-178). In curing seances and exorcisms outside of the *kerek*, ecstatic singing invokes spiritual forces and facilitates conditions for faith healing. Although the specific purpose of chanting is altered in these settings, it continues to operate as a source of social integration for the members.

Aspects of the Apostles' singing styles are not unique to the group. Other contemporary African and Afro-American cults and churches also employ didactic songs as a way of instructing members about biblical lore. Early black Christian churches in the United States used similar techniques. Jackson-Brown (1976: 36-37), for example, cites a didactic song extracted from Marshall W. Taylor's Methodist hymnal, published in Ohio in 1882. Like the Apostolic songs, Taylor's "Lis'ning All the Night" quotes and explains specific biblical passages. Although the use of ecstatic songs, both with and without instrumentation, has been widely documented for Africa's indigenous churches, the Apostolic pattern of song-chants is rare.[15]

The open format of Apostolic ceremonies provides members with appropriate moments for the social display of deep emotion. The trance-songs are both public and highly personal expressions of religious involvement. They unify the group while still fostering individual spiritual experiences. Because they rely on each member's full participation in the spiritual realities of the group, the ecstatic chants are the key to understanding Apostolic worship. Through analyzing the contexts and intensity of Apostolic ceremonial music, we can develop a new model for understanding the social dynamics of group involvement in a variety of African religious movements.

APPENDIX

I. Opening Hymns

"KWESE, KWESE"
(CHISHONA AS SUNG IN ZAMBIA AND ZIMBABWE)

Chishona	English
Kwese, kwese, tinovona vanhu hamuzivi Kristu	Everywhere, everywhere, we see people who do not know Christ
Vakarasikirwa nediko	They have lost the time
Vanomutadza muponesi	Because of sins
REFRAIN:	REFRAIN:
Mwari wedu wemasimba	Our God of strength
Tinzwe tinomukumbira	Hear us, we beg you

Chishona	English
Tumai mweya mutsvene	Send us the Holy Spirit
Kuno kune vamwe vasinawo	Here, there, where they do not have it
Vatumei mangwanani	Send them in the morning
Vatumei pamauro	Send them in the evening
Vatumei masikati	Send them in the midday
Kune misha yavo yose	To all their villages
Asi isu Baba wedu tine basa rokuita	But we, our Father, have work to do
Tine hama nesha Mwari ti	We have relatives and friends, Lord
Tumei kuna ivo	Send us to them

"MWARI KOMBORERA AFRICA"
(CHISHONA AS SUNG IN ZAMBIA AND ZIMBABWE)

Chishona	English
Mwari Komborera Africa, Alleluia	God Save Africa, Alleluia
Chisua yemina matu yedu	Hear our prayers
Mwari Baba Jesu utukomborera (Utukomborera)	God, Father, Jesus, bless us (Bless us)
Jesu, turi baranda bako	Jesus, we are your servants
REFRAIN: (Uya mueya)	REFRAIN: (Come Spirit)
O mueya, hosanna mueya, utukomborera	O come Holy Spirit, bless us
(Hosanna mueya)	(Hosanna Spirit)
O mueya, hosanna mueya, utukomborera	O come Holy Spirit, bless us
(Utukomborera)	(Bless us)
O mueya, mueya	O Holy Spirit, God, Father, Jesus, bless us
Mwari Baba Jesu, utokomborera (Utukomborera)	(Bless us)
Jesu, turi baranda bako	Jesus, we are Your servants
Aridzi mzitwe zhitarako, Alleluia	Let your name be exalted, Alleluia
Chisua yemina matu yedu, etc.	Hear our prayers, etc.
(Uya mueya), etc.	(Come Spirit), etc.
Mwari fungeni Africa, Alleluia	God remember Africa, Alleluia
Chisua yemina matu yedu, etc.	Hear our prayers, etc.
(Uya meuya), etc.	(Come Spirit), etc.
Turi pano pa rusambo rako.	We are here to meet You.

II. "Pa Kudenga:" Two Versions of Hymn Closing the Kerek (Chishona)

Methodist Hymnal*	English
Pa kudenga kuna Baba	In Heaven near the Father
Kwakanaka kwazwo	It is a good place
Pa kudenga kuna Boba	In Heaven near the Father
Kwakafara kwazwo	It is a happy place
Hakupindi chakaipa	Nothing which is bad can enter
Kanachiri chimwe	there, Nothing, even one
Hakupindi zwo kurwara	Nothing painful can enter
Ne chimwere chimwe	Nor any sickness
Ndabatswene ibo bose	They are all holy,
Banogara iko	Those who stay here
Banokuda banamate	They surpass even those who pray
Iwe Mwari wabo	You are their God
Bakawana musha wabo	They have found their home
Musha wakagara	They have seen their home
Bakawana no upenyu	They have found everlasting life
Bgusingabfubure	Which will never end
Ndiri mwenyi pane nyika	Their home to stay
Ndinosuba denga	Their good home
Ngandipinde newe Jesu	
Ndiende kudenga	I am a stranger on this earth
	I am longing for Heaven
	Let me enter with you, Jesus
	Let me go to Heaven

Apostolic**	English
Pa kudenga kuna Baba	In Heaven near the Father
Kwakanaka kwazwo	It is a good place
Pa Kudenga kuna Baba	In Heaven near the Father
Kwakafara kwazwo	It is a happy place

*This version of the "Pa Kudenga" is based upon the Methodist hymnal used in Harare, Zambabwe.

**This version of the "Pa Kudenga" is based on my tape recordings of the African Apostles, Harare, Zimbabwe.

Apostalic**	English
Hakupindi chakaipa	Nothing which is bad can enter
Kanachiri chimwe	there, Nothing, even one
Hakupindi chakurwadza	Nothing painful can enter
Nechimwere chimwe	Nor any sickness
Ndevatsvene ivo vose	They are all holy,
Vanogara uko	Those who stay here
Vanokunda vanamati	They surpass even those who pray
Iwe Mwari wavo	You are their God
Vakavona musha wavo	They have found their home
Musha wakanaka	They have seen their home
Vakavona neupenyu	They have found everlasting life
Bwuzinazoperi	Which will never end
Ndiri mwenyi paneino nyika	Their home to stay
Ndinoshuwa kudenga	Their good home
Ngandipinde newe Jesu	I am a stranger on this earth
Ndiendewo kudenga	I am longing for Heaven
	Let me enter with you, Jesus
	Let me go to Heaven

III. "Sodom and Gomorrah" (Tshiluba Text and Verses)

Tshiluba	English
Solo: Bantu, luayi ku tshiondo tshia	Solo: People, come to the drum of life, on earth is So——
muoyo, mu buloba mu So——	
All: Mu Sodomo ne Gomorrah	All: In Sodom and Gomorrah
Mu buloba mu Sodomo ne Gomorrah	On earth is Sodom and Gomorrah
Mu buloba mu Sodoma	On earth is Sodom
Solo: Jehovah Nzambi utubuikidile, mu buloba mu So——	Solo: Lord God, we call you to the earth to So——
All: Mu Sodomo ne Gomorrah	All: In Sodom and Gomorrah
Mu buloba mu Sodomo ne Gomorrah	On earth is Sodom and Gomorrah
Mu buloba mu Sodomo	On earth is Sodom

Tshiluba	English
(Similarly)	(Similarly)
Kumuedi kabobo, kena kule	Lord God pardon us
Umuele kabobo, yeye apa	If you call Him, He is
Muoyo wanyi wakujinga	not far
Nzambi wetu musela nzala	If you call Him, He is there
	My heart is longing
	Our God sought in fasting

NOTES

1. The basic research for this article was conducted from 1977 through 1979 in Lusaka, Zambia and Harare, Zimbabwe, under National Science Foundation Grant #Soc. 76-20861 and Grant #Soc. 78-20861. The study of Apostolic ceremonies was part of a larger investigation of indigenous religion and urban adjustment in Lusaka. This article was written during my tenure at the Center for Advanced Study in the Behavioral Sciences at Stanford University (1979-1980). My research at the Behavioral Sciences Center was funded by National Endowment for the Humanities Grant #FC-26278-76-1030, sponsored by the Andrew W. Mellon Foundation.

2. Cf. Murphree (1969: 94) and Jules-Rosette (1975b: 91). Apostles trace the term *kerek* or *kireke* to the Afrikaans *kerk* (church) and the Scottish word *kirk* (also church). Protestant missionaries from both of these areas were active in the southern African region during the sect's early years.

3. Cf. Daneel (1971: 320). John Maranke adapted the hymn "Kwese, Kwese" from the Shona version of the Methodist hymnal. He instructed followers to sing this song whenever they performed baptisms or initiated preaching and prayer. The "Mwari" was to be used for opening full worship services. The Apostolic texts of these hymns are included in the appendix.

4. Contrasting versions of the *"Mwari"* have been used by political leaders. This hymn is also known as the "African Anthem." Woods (1978: 8) presents the following translation of verses from the political version of the anthem: "God bless Africa / Raise up her spirit / Hear our prayers / And bless us." The Apostles sing this tune more slowly and solemnly.

5. There are four ranks in the Apostolic church: baptiser or pastor, evangelist or preacher, prophet, and healer. Within these ranks, there are three leadership grades, distinguished by the titles *Lieb-Ummah, L-U,* and *L*—(meaning "he who speaks with God"). Women do not hold the *Lieb-*

Ummah grades of leadership. They may, however, hold the ranks of prophetess and healer (cf. Aquina, 1967: 203-209).

6. The conflict between Musumbu and Nawezi, two elder baptizers in the Zairean church, resulted in the latter's excommunication for political reasons. An effort was made to stabilize the semiautonomous branches of the Zairean Apostles by appointing Musumbu as their major representative to the Zimbabwean church center. I have discussed these political disputes at more length elsewhere (Jules-Rosette, 1979: 109-136).

7. Jones (1959) discusses the contrast between Western pentatonic scales and African scales. Apostolic vocal parts are almost all in major tonality. The harmonies produced stay closest to diatonic chord singing, adapted from the mission churches. At the same time, Apostolic harmonies also reflect customary African influences. Parallel fourths and fifths and canons at the fourth or fifth occur frequently. Frequent modal constraints include avoiding the seventh and the use of parallel thirds among Zambian Apostles. There are, however, significant regional variations in Apostolic harmonies.

8. Further verses and improvisations upon "Sodom and Gomorrah" have been recorded by Haldor Heimer (1971: 456-459) and Lanzas and Bernard (1966: 189-216). This song appears to be Zairean (in particular, Luba) in origin, although it is now sung in several Apostolic regional congregations across Central Africa. The process of adopting successful songs from one congregation and spreading them to others is a common practice at church conferences.

9. Chernoff (1979: 91-151) discusses the importance of drumming and dance styles in African music. While the Apostles forbid the actual use of drums, they create the incessant rhythmic background of percussives through the *ngoma* vocalizations. Dancing is replaced by swaying either in the standing or in the seated position during *kerek* and curing services.

10. Cf. Kilson (1971: 58-97). Kilson presents a large collection of ritual variations on song texts used for Ghanaian divination. Apostles similarly innovate their praise songs. The calls to obey the law have punitive implications and are often directed at outsiders and backsliders within the congregation.

11. Cf. Jules-Rosette (1977: 210-215). Maranke Apostles at this joint ceremony accused their guests of singing "like toads"! They meant that the outsiders did not share their understanding of ecstatic songs and their spiritual fervor. Nevertheless, the features of Apostolic singing are so distinctive that Masowe members followed and imitated their hosts easily. Singing in this case served as a means of maintaining boundaries between the two groups.

12. It is for this reason that nonmembers are not considered capable of

singing Apostolic songs appropriately. Songs unify the group in the face of outsiders. At the same time, singing is a major technique of Apostolic proselytizing.

13. If the conflicts and criticisms aired in songs were presented in discourse, church judges would have to intervene to resolve the conflicts. The medium of song removes conflicts from the immediate political and judicial domain of church leadership.

14. The cathartic effect of Apostolic music is manifest in ecstatic singing during *kerek* and healing and exorcism seances. At the termination of ecstatic singing, a sense of calm pervades the congregation. An emotional reaction is one of the goals of this chanting.

15. Sundkler (1961: 192-198) presented one of the earliest analyses of the hymns and sacred dances of South African indigenous churches. He describes the musical innovation, borrowing, and the process of improvisation in Zulu Zionist churches and notes the importance of modifications on traditional drumming and dancing among South African cultists.

REFERENCES

Aquina, Sister Mary, O.P. 1967. "The People of the Spirit: An Independent Church in Rhodesia." *Africa*, 37 (2).

Barrett, David. 1968. *Schism and Renewal in Africa: An Analysis of Six Thousand Contemporary Religious Movements.* Nairobi: Oxford University Press.

Chernoff, John Miller. 1979. *African Rhythm and African Sensibility.* Chicago: University of Chicago Press.

Daneel, Marthinus L. 1971. *The Old and New in Southern Shona Independent Churches.* Vol. I. The Hague: Mouton.

Heimer, Haldor. 1971. "The Kimbanguists and the Bapostolo: A Study of Two Independent Churches in Luluabourg, Congo in Relation to Similar Churches and in the Context of Lulua Traditional Culture and Religion." Ph.D. dissertation, Hartford Seminary Foundation.

Jackson-Brown, Irene V. 1976. "Afro-American Song in the Nineteenth Century: A Neglected Source." *The Black Perspective in Music*, 4, 1, Spring.

Jones, A. M. 1959. *Studies in African Music.* Vol. I. London: Oxford University Press.

Jules-Rosette, Bennetta. 1975a. *African Apostles: Ritual and Conversion in the Church of John Maranke.* Ithaca: Cornell University Press.

_____. 1975b. "Bapostolo Ritual: An African Response to Christianity." *Canadian Journal of African Studies*, 8, Fall.

_____. 1975c. "Song and Spirit: The Use of Song in the Management of Ritual Settings." *Africa*, 45 (2).

_____. 1977. "Grass-Roots Ecumenism: Religious and Social Cooperation in Two African Churches." *African Social Research*, 23, June.

_____. 1979. "Prophecy and Leadership in the Maranke Church: A Case Study of Continuity and Change." In *African Christianity: Patterns of Religious Continuity* eds. George Bond, Sheila Walker, and Walton Johnson. New York: Academic Press.

Kilson, Marion. 1971. *Kpele Lala: Ga Religious Songs and Symbols*. Cambridge, Massachusetts: Harvard University Press.

Lanzas, A. and Guy Bernard. 1966. "Les Fidèles d'Une Nouvelle Eglise au Congo." *Genêve-Afrique: Acta Africana*, 5: 189-216.

Lomax, Alan. 1970. "The Homogeneity of African Afro-American Musical Style." In *Afro-American Anthropology*, ed. by Whitten, N. W. and Szwed, J. F. New York: The Free Press.

Maranke, John. 1953. *The New Witness of the Apostles*. Bocha, Rhodesia. (Mimeographed volume).

Murphree, Marshall W. 1969. *Christianity and the Shona*. London: The Athlone Press.

Schutz, Afred. 1964. "Making Music Together." *Collected Papers*. Vol. II. The Hague: Martinus Nijhoff.

Sundkler, B.G.M. 1961. *Bantu Prophets in South Africa*. London: International African Institute.

Walker, Sheila S. 1972. *Ceremonial Spirit Possession in Africa and Afro-America*. Leiden, Holland: E. J. Brill.

Woods, Donald. 1978. *Biko*. New York: Paddington Press Ltd.

A Yoruba/Nagô "Melotype" for Religious Songs in the African Diaspora: Continuity of West African Praise Song in the New World

In this chapter, I present an updated perspective on the analytical study of songs of the Afro-Bahian Ketu cult completed in 1951 by the late Alan P. Merriam. Specifically, I examine Merriam's comment that no model exists for the "structure of Yoruba music." Although work did begin on Nigeria and Brazil during the 1950s at Northwestern University, where Merriam completed his doctoral dissertation, he claims that *comparative* musical data from Nigeria and Brazil was unavailable at the time of his study.[1]

Almost twenty years later, I was eager to do field research among the Yoruba of southwestern Nigeria. In 1970-71, I collected twenty hours of Shango (the Yoruba god of thunder and lightning) music. I transcribed selected pieces and translated them into English, giving me a musical data base for this discourse. My subsequent fieldwork in Haiti (1973) and Bahia (1979-80) has revealed that apparently a melodic "nucleus" has been retained in Black cultures throughout the New World—particularly those where Yoruba descendants have faithfully held on to their heritage for several centuries. I am borrowing the term nucleus from Erich von Hornbostel (1928: 24), who observed that African song texts inherently employ a particular type of vocal rendition that is "tonal" in nature. I will refer to this nucleus as a "melotype."[2] I will focus on three cultural areas that share a common heritage of West African religious beliefs and practices: Yorubaland in southwestern Nigeria, Bahia in northeastern Brazil, and Haiti in the Caribbean. Among the Yoruba, the tie to the homeland is most emphatically demonstrated. It is possible that the melotype, a linking element among these groups, came to the New World with the introduction of the Yoruba slave trade more than three centuries ago.

AFRO/BAHIAN RELIGION AND THE YORUBA SLAVE TRADE

With the advent of the slave trade to Bahia, Black communities have retained a wealth of their West African heritage in the form of *candomblé*—a rich complex of religious beliefs, especially Yoruba mythology, song, dance, and spectacle.

Bahia may well be the purest center of neo-African "traditional" religion. It has more *terreiros* (literally, sacred grounds) than any other part of Brazil—and probably any other Black community in the New World. Slaves were brought from different regions of Africa to both North and South America. Baptized, and obliged to adopt rules and patterns of living agreeable to their master's religious principles, they ran the risk of losing all their traditions and individuality. As ethnologist Pierre Verger (1964: 2) explains: "Bahia is one of the few places in the New World where this alienation was not complete, and where certain African traditions, Yoruba ones in particular, have been successfully maintained in spite of adverse circumstances."

Ethnological studies of Afro-Brazilian religion derived, in turn, from West African and Congo beliefs and practices. Studies have been undertaken by Brazilian scholars only since the turn of the century. For eighty years, Western scholars have maintained an interest in Afro-Brazilian religion. Nina Rodrigues (1932), Herskovits (1941), and Verger (1957) were among the first to take an interest in the West African origins of these religious traditions, particularly those of the Yoruba, who have lived for centuries in urban towns in southwestern Nigerian and parts of Dahomey. Pierson (1942), Carneiro (1954), Verger (1957), Bastide (1958, 1967, 1978), and others have published a great deal of information on the worship of Yoruba gods in Bahia. Xangô,[3] the Yoruba god of thunder and lightning, is most frequently identified with the Roman Catholic Saint Jerome and Oiá, his most faithful wife and goddess of winds and storms, with Saint Barbara. In traditional

Yoruba religion, Ṣango is said to have ruled over the ancient Ọyọ empire; Yoruba mythology and praise songs abound with references to his colorful personality and brazen, magical deeds:

> The strong medicine-man who lives both
>   in trees and in bushes,
> He swells with wealth and pageantry.
> The lightning which transforms the sky
>   into a fiery, blinding one. . . .
>   (Verger 1957: 340ff)

Nina Rodrigues (1932) has called Xangô the most popular orixá (or deity) in Bahian myths, which tell how Xangô pursued Oiá to the palace of Olokun, the sea goddess, fled Ọyọ, and hanged himself (Bascom, 1972: 7-8). Despite the wealth of data on the deities, very little ethnomusicology has been done in Bahia, among Nagô communities. Present-day communities are descendants of Blacks brought over from the mid-seventeenth to the mid-nineteenth centuries by Atlantic slave traders.

My study concerns the vocal rendition of Ṣango praise-poetry and song that I first observed among the Yoruba (Welch 1972). These renditions are representative of a particular religious music/ oral poetic genre that has been preserved in Bahia. It is my primary objective in this discourse to show how Yoruba musical/cultural traits have survived in Bahian *candomblé* religious ceremonies. Isolating one type of West African religious music—Ṣango praise poetry —I traced its diffusion to one New World Bahian religious center, where it is rendered during the annual festival (*Festa*) for Xangô. Through this tradition, the rich heritage from the "Old World" manifests itself in the modern world and binds a group in mutual faith and understanding.

Since at least 1830—when the first Nagô candomblé in Bahia was officially recorded—West African traditions have been a colorful, dynamic contribution to Brazilian culture as a whole. The Nagô (originally of the Ketu and Ọyọ "nations" in Yorubaland) still sing songs in the "African" dialect—with some modification, owing to the nature of oral transmission and the fact that Yoruba is no longer spoken on a day-to-day basis.

Now, let us turn to the Nagô *candomblé* and explore their general pattern within which the melotype takes shape.

NAGÔ CANDOMBLÉ AND "TRADITIONAL" HIERARCHY AND PROTOCOL

Candomblé is the general term used in Bahia to designate a religious ceremony, cult, or religion that originated in Africa. Blacks who were brought from Africa to the Americas belonged to different "nations" (for example, Nagô, Angola, Dahomey, Ashanti, and so forth), each "nation" having its own language, tradition, and divinities. Nagô *candomblé* is "pure-African," which contrasts with other contemporary eclectic cults in Bahia. In Bahia, registered candomblés number over 900 and candomblé exerts a powerful influence over Brazilian culture. *Candomblé*, a monotheistic cult, is a neo-African religion in which devotees worship a supreme being called *Olorum*. This supreme being is a deity who rules through subsidiary divinities called *orixás*. *Orixás* are the deities to whom devotees appeal for help in winning love, curing sickness, and strengthening levels of endurance. The *orixás* are worshipped in various cults known in different regions in Brazil as *candomblé, macumba, bataque, para,* or simply *xangô*. The latter, xangô, is found along the northern coast, especially in Pernambuco. As in other syncretic cults in the New World,[4] Yoruba *orişa* have been identified with Roman Catholic saints. These syncretisms, however, are not consistent and vary from one area to another, even from cult house to cult house.

The Nagô have upheld Yoruba ancestral traditions most faithfully. Nagô divinities are worshipped in temples called *terreiros,* generally found on the outskirts of the city proper (São Salvador da Bahia). The *terreiro* contains the *peji*, where altars of the divinities are found and the *barracão,* a large room for public ceremonies. Also in this sacred place are smaller houses for several important *orixás,* that receive annual offerings and are worshipped during special events. There are also the *camarinha,* a secluded room where initiates stay before "receiving the *orixá*" and a sacred tree (*iroko*) on the premises.

Spiritual responsibilities of the cult come under the *Pai-de-santo* (high priest) or the *Mãe-de-santo* (high priestess). She has ultimate control over the entire *candomblé* community and all ceremonial events. She may also be the caretaker of the *axé*, which gives the spiritual aura to the *terreiro*. In the event of her illness or incapacity to carry out her functions as superior authority, the *mãe pequena* who is secondary in importance takes over. Then come the *filhas-de-*

santo, the initiated ones; they are followed by the *ekedes*, "servants" of the *orixá* who care for the costumes and ornaments; and, finally, the *abian*, those who have fulfilled only partial rites for their initiation. The hierarchy is based on that of the Nagô's African ancestors. The men's roles essentially involve occasional honorary functions. There is the *peji-gan*, master of the altar; the *axogum*, who is in charge of sacrificing the animals; the *ogans*, protectors who give prestige to the community and perform material responsibilities (such as offering money); and finally, the *alabê*, who directs the drummers in the *atabaque* (drumming) ensemble.

In the Yoruba conception, the *orixás*, in primordial times, were like Xangô (Ṣango), privileged human beings who possessed powers over certain phenomena of nature. When they died, they became rivers, rocks, trees, and lakes. Descendants of the *orixás* continue the cult of their divinized predecessors and serve as intermediaries between the *orixás* and the forces of nature, which they control. The most traditional devotees of *candomblé* worship these *orixás* or natural spirits (water, wind, rain, thunder, rainbow, leaves, et cetera). While ritual varies, most often it takes the form of dances, which mime the major adventures, deeds, and traits of these *orixás*, vividly reflected in Yoruba/Nagô mythology.

During public ceremonies, the *barracão* is decorated with paper streamers, associated with the colors of the *orixá* who is being paid homage. In the foreground is the drumming ensemble (*atabaque*), consisting of three drums of graduated sizes—the *rum*, *rumpi*, and *le*—along with the traditional *agogo*, a double-iron bell, which maintains a steady beat, according to the particular dances performed. The *alabê* plays this bell to "announce" the beginning of the ceremony. His calls are to summon the *orixás* to the celebration. Each *orixá* responds to a particular rhythm pattern. For example, the rhythm for Xangô, called *alujá*, is a steady frenetic rhythmic pattern which continually grows in intensity. After the obligatory homage to Exú (the god who "stands at the crossroads"), called *padê*, the *filhas-de-santo* dance in a circle, singing three or four songs for each *orixá*. These are songs of praise (*oriki*) which describe each god's temperament and personality. During the dancing and singing, the *orixás* "descend" on their "children," who become possessed and pass into trance, at which time they are carried out of the room. After all the *orixás* have descended, they return in a group procession, clothed in ritual costume. One by one, they display their particular characteristics and mime their feats and deeds. Finally, the *orixás* are expelled by a series of songs. Often, a communal feast follows, during which participants share the ritual meal of the *orixá* being honored.

Xangô is a powerful *orixá* in Nagô *candomblé*:

Xango is the divinity of thunder and lightning and is symbolized by lightning stones, a dance wand (*oxé*), and a metal rattle (*xeré*) . . . syncretized with Saint Jerome. His colors are white and red; his sacred day is Wednesday and when he is ritually "fed," his favorite dish is *amalá*, an okra stew. Xangô's sacrificial foods also include goats, chickens and a type of turtle. Xangô's dance is war-like—virile and dignified [he was once a king of the Ọyọ empire]. His salutation or ritual greeting is *Kawo Kabiesile!* (Hail, Your Majesty!). Bascom 1972: 10)

The most spectacular aspect of the candomblé ritual is the trance. Ramos (1951: 97) describes the *orixá's* possession of the initiate in this way:

Movements, gyrations and contortions [occur], at first as a rhythmical, graceful dance, becoming progressively more intense, more violent, going on tirelessly until the final spasmodic manifestation—possession itself— when the *orixá* descends and "mounts" the *filha-de-santo*; . . . often violent physical expressions accompany convulsions which indicate the entrance of the *orixá* into the body, at which time the group pays honor and reference to the new initiates.

The psychological effect of the trance phenomenon deserves an entire separate study which the present essay cannot expect to tackle.

PRAISE-POETRY

Where word meaning depends on lexical tones, accents, and glides—although literal meanings of Yoruba praise-poetry (*oriki*) may have been forgotten—the significance or general purpose of the *oriki* is alive in the minds of Nagô devotees. Just as dance and music are intertwined, so text is perceived as an integral part of the ritual, as are all the other elements of ritual expression—gestures, ritual objects, and symbols. As one Bahian scholar stated:

There is no dichotomization in Nagô ritual; the religious community is one of synthesis, whose dialectics are functional and dynamic. . . . Interrelated elements complement each other in complex patterns, as the rite is a symbol where nothing is gratuitous—every element is integral to the whole. Thus, music/cum/text are not perceived as separate entities, but as a vital part of the gestalt of the rite. (Dos Santos 1980)

Thus, to the outsider, the ritual appears to be chanting and singing, but for the carriers of the tradition, it is an act of invocation and praise. Ritual poetry is intoned in a mode that will appease the divinities and cause them to respond favorably. To the performer, text and mode of intonation are inseparable. While many Yoruba texts have been unconsciously altered or transformed through time as they are transmitted orally from generation to generation, what is important is that they still retain their ritual significance to members of the community—and to the divinities to whom the praises are addressed.

Despite the fact that worshippers may not know the significance of each Yoruba name or town or historical/mythological event that occurred in a "mysterious place" called Africa, devotees know when the praise is intended for a particular deity; in Nagô practice, the sequence of songs is ritually prescribed. In any case, most important is the spiritual communication, the welcoming of the African *orixá* to the sacred space of the *terreiro* to join with the other *orixás* in the celebration of the *Festa*.

THE MELOTYPE AS A CULTURAL SURVIVOR IN NAGÔ *CANDOMBLÉ*

This section of the essay will attempt to show that the "melotype" might well be a connecting link that demonstrates the cultural continuity between Yoruba religion in southwestern Nigeria and Dahomey and traditional Nagô *candomblé* in Bahia.

The word *melotype* is derived from two Greek words that describe the indigenous Yoruba religious praise song: (1) *melopeia*, a form of declamation or chant built around one tone or pitch, and (2) *melodia*, literally, choral song. The "pitch vocabulary" is derived from the tonal structure of the original West African language, Yoruba (see figure 9.1). The sound pattern was originally associated with precise inflections inherent in the language's linguistic traits. It thus involved three levels of the vocal register —low, middle, and high. What has persisted is a combination of pitches centered around a feeling of "tonality" which approximates our concept of the triad in Western functional harmony: I-III-V in minor and major modes (see figure 9.2). Thus, altered forms of the "melotype" allow for flexibility in the overall sound pattern.

If we consider the melotype within a dorian modal framework, we have the pitches D-F-A as our fundamental tonality, with G and C occurring sporadically in the melodic pattern. (D also occurs an octave higher as an extension.) When these same pitches are rearranged in ascending sequence, we have the pentatonic vocabulary of many songs in the Yoruba Şango repertoire (that is, D-F-G-A-C-[D]) (see figure 9.2). I found that the majority of the forty-seven Sango songs and chants I collected in Yorubaland operated within this pitch framework. Nearly all (87 percent) conformed to a triadic pattern, with minor triads prevailing over major.

Several other parameters appear to typify the Yoruba Şango songs; a predominance of narrow and medium intervals—minor third (m3), major second (M2), and major third (M3); a descending (in 53 percent of the songs) or level (in 44 percent of the songs) line contour or melodic direction; and the use of sequence, a common device in 53 percent of the thirty-four songs I analyzed.

These Yoruba music traits appear in many Xangô songs within the Bahian repertoire. Many orixás are invoked during candomblé, and these same musical features might be recognized as well in songs for Xangô's wives—Oxum, Iansã (Oiá) and Oba (Euá). (In Yorubaland, each of these female orixás has a separate cult dedicated to her.) But, in this essay, I must limit my analysis to praise songs for Xangô.

I would like to stress that it is not so important that individual songs or texts from Brazil and the Caribbean be recognized as coming from Oyo in Nigeria or Ketu in Dahomey; nor is it crucial that every word still be understood or translated literally. Rather, the important point is that the ritual events with which these songs are connected and the melotype embodied within them have endured to the present day in traditional Nagô communities. With the melotype, mental musical structure has been preserved, a structure which may have existed in Bahia for as long as fifteen generations (see figures 9.3, 9.4, and 9.5).

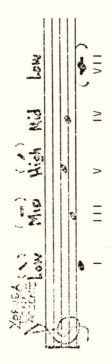

Figure 9.1 Yoruba tonal accents

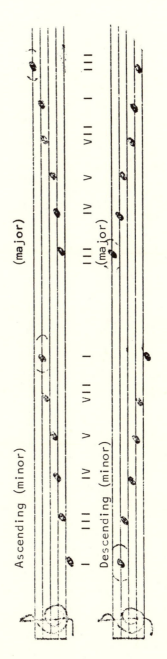

Figure 9.2 The candomblé melotype

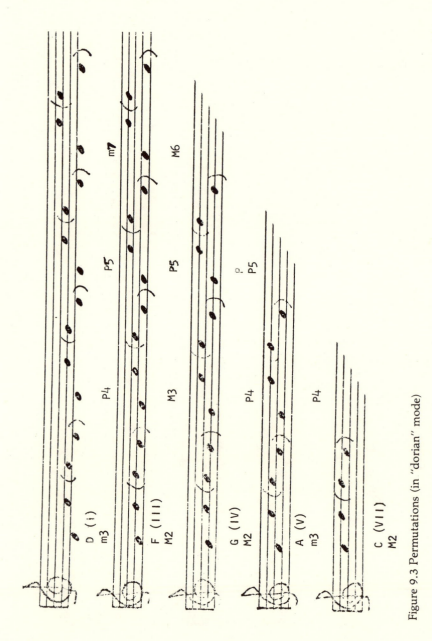

Figure 9.3 Permutations (in "dorian" mode)

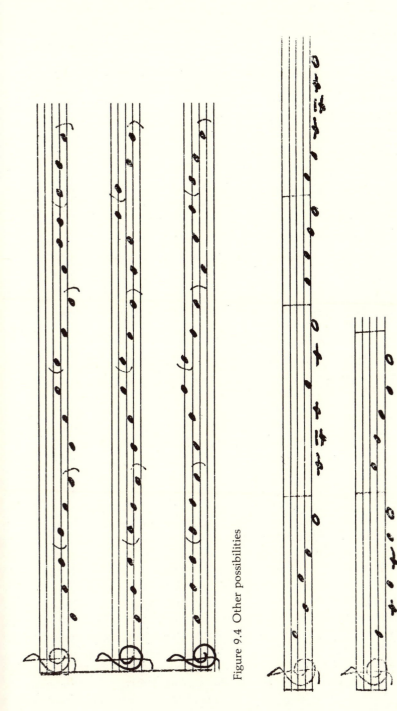

Figure 9.4 Other possibilities

Figure 9.5 Cadences (from Yoruba songs)

Expanding Merriam's analysis of twenty-nine Ketu (Nagô) songs (collected by Melville J. Herskovits in 1941/42), I found the following musical traits were descriptive of the songs which, in turn, demonstrate the melotype (see figure 9.6):

1. a medium or wide tonal range
2. a downward melodic direction
3. a predominance of Major second (M2) and minor third (m3) intervals with the Major third (M3) next in importance
4. a prevalence of syncopated and offbeat patterns
5. a pentatonic scalar pattern with conspicuous absence of the semitone
6. percussion instrument tones falling on I, V, IV, and III of the mode (figures 9.3 and 9.4)
7. a well-defined tonality
8. overlap occurring in a leader-chorus relationship, with the leader "lining out" the refrain for the chorus
9. frequent ornamentation
10. a steady, ongoing tempo, also well-defined
11. an extremely important percussion rhythm, polymetric with extensive elaboration of distinct motives

All of these traits can be found in the musical examples provided here—especially the triadic melotype. (See figures 9.6, 9.7, 9.8, 9.9, 9.10)

CONCLUSION

Over thirty years ago (Merriam 1951) discovered that Nagô songs exhibit African patterns—so strongly as to leave no doubt whatsoever of the relationship between Ketu (Nagô), and West African styles. "The relationship," Merriam (1956: 64-65) maintains, "seems incontrovertible." By comparing the above examples of songs and chants from Yoruba, Haitian, and Bahian religious communities, we can see that an established cultural link has survived within musical types in the African Diaspora. Songs praising the same deity (Ṣango = Xangô = Changó) share common musical traits, attesting to the fact that when Blacks were brought to Bahia, they brought a valuable part of their cultural heritage; their mental awareness and cognizance of their traditional African songs served

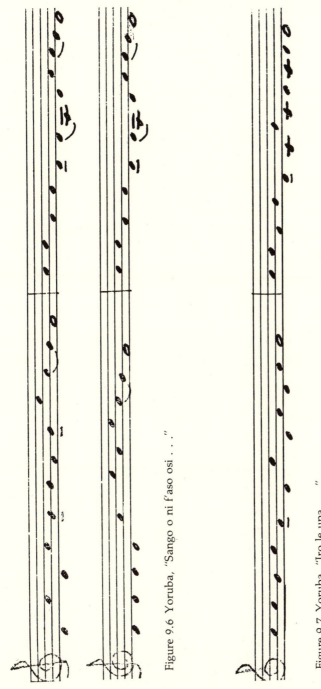

Figure 9.6 Yoruba, "Sango o ni f'aso osi . . . "

Figure 9.7 Yoruba, "Iro le upa . . . "

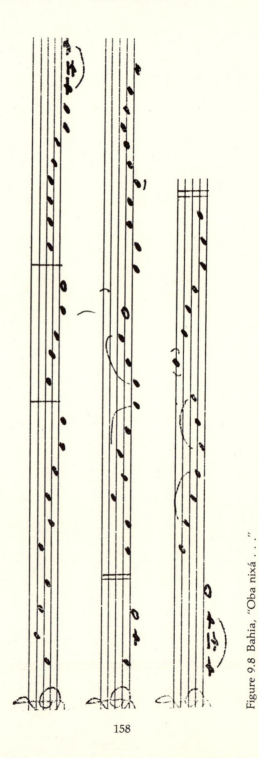

Figure 9.8 Bahia, "Oba nixá . . ."

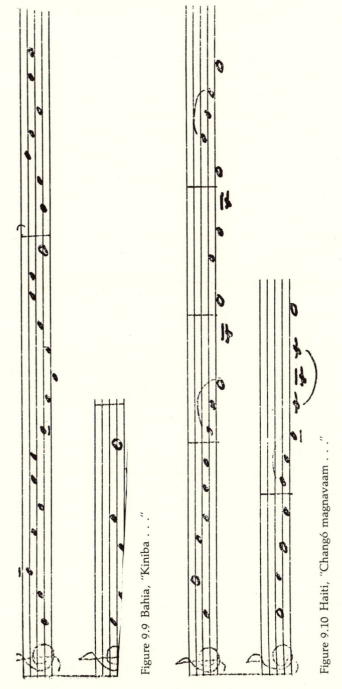

Figure 9.9 Bahia, "Kiniba . . ."

Figure 9.10 Haiti, "Changó magnavaam . . ."

—perhaps unconsciously—as a model for "recreating" songs in the New World.

The melotype is an aural indicator of continuity within the African Diaspora. Such additional musical phenomena as the "unstable third," descending and ascending glides, a quavering voice quality and general pitch flexibility might be recognized as further evidence of traditional West African vocal style and mannerism in the music of the New World.

NOTES

1. Merriam's ethnomusicological analysis was a pioneer effort to describe Nagô songs collected in Bahia, Brazil, in 1941-42 by Melville J. Herskovits.

2. The phenomenon ("melotype") discussed in this discourse was first recognized in Port-au-Prince, Haiti, where a Changó song was discovered which was astonishingly similar to the Ṣango songs collected in Yorubaland (see figure 9.10). Although Changó is considered subservient to Ogoun in the loá pantheon, the song was strongly Yoruba in character.

3. Throughout the text, orthography follows standard written convention for the respective languages—Yoruba, Portuguese, and French, that is s = x = ch (ex. oriṣa = orixá = orichá; Ṣango = Xangô = Changó).

4. It is significant to note that in Trinidad, as in Pernambuco, Brazil, shango is the name of the cult in which the Yoruba gods, known as "powers," are worshipped in much the same manner as in candomblé. Xangô is also the god of thunder and lightning and retains many of the traits associated with him in Bahia; in Haiti, where Yoruba descendants are known as Nagô or Anago, the dominant African deities, called loá, are the vodun of the Fon of Dahomey, worshipped in the vodoun or "voodoo" cult. It is Sogbo who is believed to cause thunder. Ṣhango, also known, is considered a servant of Ogoun, god of war; and in Cuba, descendants of Yoruba slaves are known as lucumi. Yoruba gods are known as oricha or santos, and their worship is known as santería. As in Haiti and Trinidad, many similar characteristics and especially Yoruba myths can be found. Consult Ortiz (1950, 1951) and Cabrera (1954) for further information on the above. See also Bascom (1972: 10-123).

REFERENCES

The following is a list of books relevant to this study. References to Yoruba and Bahian religion—as well as mention of related materials on vaudou in Haiti and santería in Cuba are included here.

Bascom, W. 1969. *The Yoruba of Southwestern Nigeria*. New York: Holt, Rinehart & Winston.

_____. 1972. *Ṣhango in the New World*. Occasional Publication of the African and Afro-American Research Institute. Austin: University of Texas.

Bastide, R. 1958. *Le candomblé de Bahia: rite nago*. Paris.

_____. 1967. *Les Amériques noires*. Paris: Editions Payot.

_____. 1978. *The African Religions of Brazil*. Baltimore, Md.: Johns Hopkins University Press.

Cabrera, L. 1954. *El Monte*. La Habana, Cuba.

Carneiro, E. 1954. *Candomblés da Bahia*. Bahia: Publicacões do Museu do Estado, 8.

Courlander, H. 1960. *The Drum and the Hoe*. Berkeley & Los Angeles: University of California Press.

Ellis, A. B. 1894. *The Yoruba-Speaking Peoples of the Slave Coast of West Africa*. London: Chapman & Hall.

Gleason, J. 1971. *Orisha: The Gods of Yorubaland*. New York: Atheneum.

Gonzales-Wipper, M. 1973. *Santería: African Magic in Latin America*. New York: Julian Press.

Herskovits, M. J. 1937. *The Myth of the Negro Past*. New York: Harper Bros.

Hornbostel, Erich Von. 1928. *African Negro Music Africa*. Vol. 1.

Idowu, E. G. 1962. *Olodumare, God in Yoruba Belief*. London: Longman.

Johnson, S. 1921. *The History of the Yorubas*. London: Routledge & Sons.

Merriam, A. P. 1951. "Songs of the Afro-Bahian Ketu cult: An Ethnomusicological Analysis." Ph.D. dissertation, Northwestern University.

_____. 1956. "Songs of the Ketu Cult of Bahia, Brazil." *African Music*, Vol. 1, No. 3.

Nina Rodrigues, R. 1932. *Os africanos no Brasil*. São Paulo: Cia Editora Nacional.

Ojo, G.J.S. 1967. *Yoruba Culture*. Ile-Ife: University of Ife.

Ortiz, F. 1950. *La Africania de la Música Folklorica de Cuba*. La Habana: Ediciones Cardeans y Cia.

_____. 1951. *Los Bailes y el Teatro do los Negros en el Folklore de Cuba*. La Habana: ediciones Carenas y Cia.

Pierson, D. 1942. *Negroes in Brazil*. Chicago: University of Chicago Press.

Ramos, A. 1951. *The Negro in Brazil*. New York: Dryden Press.

Roberts, J. S. 1972. *Black Music in Two Worlds*. New York: Praeger.

Santos, J. E. dos. 1975. *Os Nagô e a Morte*. Petropolis: Editora Vozes.

_____. 1980. Interview, Bahia, Brazil, April.

Simpson, G. E. 1965a. "The Ṣhango Cult in Trinidad." *African Notes*, III, 1.

_____. 1965b. "The Vodun Cult in Haiti." *African Notes*, III, 2.

162   David B. Welch

_____. 1970. *Religious Cults of the Caribbean: Trinidad, Jamaica and Haiti*. Rio Pedras, Puerto Rico: University of Puerto Rico Institute of Caribbean Studies.

Verger, P. 1957. *Notes sur le culte des orisa et vodun*. Dakar: IFAN, (Memoire, 51).

_____. 1964. *Bahia and the West African Slave Trade: 1549-1851*. Ibadan: Ibadan University Press.

Welch, D. B. 1972. "Aspects of Vocal Performance in Sango Priase-Poetry and Song." Ph.D. dissertation, Northwestern University.

They Sing with the Voice of the Drum: Afro-Panamanian Musical Traditions

It is becoming more and more evident to scholars that within the diversity that characterizes musical styles of Black societies in the Americas, there exists a unity, which is far more important. Common aesthetic values and a striking similarity in performance techniques, overall style, and expressive focus predominate, even though regional and structural differences seem to separate various groups. Focusing on this unity affords the serious student a broader understanding of the growth, development, and cultural adaptation of Blacks as a group in the Americas. A careful examination of shared historical, cultural, and political realities must be integrated into any meaningful study of expressive behavior.

Although Panama has not received a great deal of attention from researchers in sociology, anthropology and, especially, the arts, the literature on Panama is growing steadily and contributing to our overall understanding of Black culture.

Historical, demographical, and geographical characteristics place Panama firmly within the context of circum-Caribbean studies. The isthmus of Panama, shaped like a flattened S on its side, lies at the southeast extremity of Central America. The center of the republic is located at 9°N and 81°W on the shores of Lake Gatun in the province of Colon. Totaling only 29,209 square miles and extending from east to west some 420 miles, Panama varies in width from 31.5 to 113 miles. Extending the length of the country is a spine of mountains, which forms the continental divide and from which some 300 rivers emanate. The warm waters of the Caribbean Sea bathe the coast to the north, while the capital and provinces to the south look out upon the quiet Pacific ocean. Within the extensive Gulf of Panama, some fifty miles southeast of Panama City, lies the archipelago of Las Perlas. The largest island, Isla del Rey (Island of the King), is historically important, for it was the site of one of the earliest slave rebellions in the sixteenth century and the home of Filipillo, a Cimarron king.

THE AFRICAN PRESENCE IN PANAMA

Sometimes called "the bridge of the world," Panama was the focus of traffic in African slaves from the sixteenth to the mid-eighteenth centuries. During the colonial era, slaves were brought directly from Africa and Caribbean plantations to work in Panama. In addition, English- and French-speaking Blacks from Jamaica, Barbados, Martinique, Guadeloupe, Saint Kitts, Saint Lucia, and other Caribbean islands came to build the transisthmian railroad and interoceanic canal.

In Panama today, these groups are represented by their descendants. Social scientists working in the area have coined special terms for them. Descendants of the earlier slaves from Africa and Caribbean plantations, as well as the Cimarrones who fled to the jungles of eastern Panama, are referred to as *Negro Mestizo* (Torres 1975: 287) or, more commonly, *Afro-Colonial*. These people are predominantly Spanish-speaking and most often have Spanish surnames. The descendants of the railroad and canal workers are called *Afro-Antillanos* (Antillian Negroes). Practically speaking, however, it is now often difficult to discern which group a person belongs to since there has been intermarriage and other sociocultural contact for more than 150 years.

According to statistics published by the United Nations, out of an estimated population of 1,887,000 in 1980, 9 percent were designated white; 70 percent were mestizo (this total might well include the mulatto group); 14 percent were African Negro (it is not clear whether or not this number refers to peoples with little or no racial mixing); and 7 percent were Indian.

This study will focus on the musical traditions of the Afro-

Coloniales; the assimilation of non-Hispanic peoples and their traditions must await future investigation. I will concentrate here on those settlements that illuminate the most characteristic elements of Afro-Colonial expressive culture.

Figure 10.1 shows exact locations of cities and towns.

The regions that are of greatest importance to our discussion may be divided into four geographical sections:

1. Caribbean coastal area (Province of Colón): Colón, Portobelo, María Chiquita, Piña, Salud, Palenque, and Palmas Bellas

2. Provinces of Panama and Cocle: Panama City, Chepo, La Chorrera, Penonomé, and Antón

3. Archipelago of Las Pelas: Isla del Rey (San Miguel)

4. Province of Darién: Garachiné and Tucutí

Geographic groupings, though convenient for locating musical phenomena, should not be construed to mean musical style areas. There is both homogeneity and vital diversity within each region. Subtle variations add to the flavor of regional musical performance. The reader also should be aware that the focus here is not simply on retentions from specific African tribes or religious rituals. As Bastide (1969: 14) so succinctly points out, "America offers us an extraordinary picture of the rupture of ethnicity and culture."[1] Thus, connections are more general in nature; "derived" forms and practices equally claim our attention.

A time span of some four hundred years, along with ambiguous records, precludes a measure of certainty. While it is clear that some early Cimarron kings such as Filipillo (a latino), Luí de Mozambique, and Antón Mandinga had definite ethnic identities, there does not seem to be a direct correspondence in retention of specific tribal beliefs or practices from the areas that are indicated by their names. Research to date has not solved these questions. Further, as Bastide (1969: 14) points out, "it is without doubt that in the beginning, slaves of the cities and free negroes were grouped into 'Nations' with their kings and governors." These "nations" were named after places and tribes in Africa (generally from the west coast and Central Africa)—for example, Carabalí, Mandinga, Mozambiques, Andra, Angola, and Congo (1969: 15).

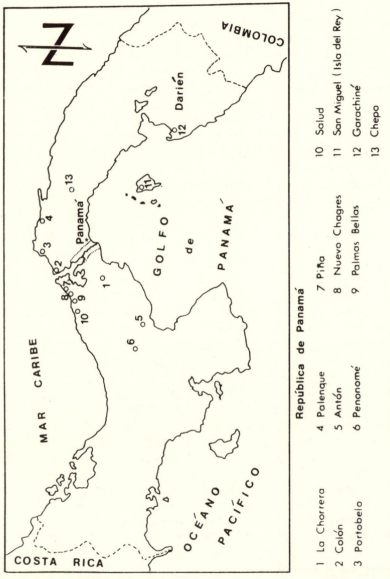

República de Panamá

1 La Chorrera	4 Palenque	7 Piña
2 Colón	5 Antón	8 Nuevo Chagres
3 Portobelo	6 Penonomé	9 Palmas Bellas

10 Salud	
11 San Miguel (Isla del Rey)	
12 Garachiné	
13 Chepo	

Figure 10.1 Map of centers of Afro-Colonial culture

HISTORY

In the New World, "gold, glory, and evangelism was the trilogy of basic impulses which motivated the actions of the Conquistadores" (Guillot n.d.: 13). Panama's strategic geographical location made it a unique jewel in Spain's overseas empire. Merchants, explorers, adventurers, and Catholic clergy were all attracted to Panama early in the sixteenth century.

Not until his fourth voyage to the New World did Columbus actually traverse the Caribbean coast of Panama, arriving at the westernmost end in the laguna of Chiriquí. It was in 1502 in the central provinces—then called *Veraguas* by the indigenous inhabitants—that Columbus first encountered reports of great wealth and gold. Through barter with the Indians, he obtained a few golden trinkets and some jewelry. Intent on discovering a western passage to the East Indies, Columbus sailed eastward along the isthmus until he discovered an Indian village, on the shores of a beautiful harbor, which he named Portobelo (Arce 1911: 44-46). Failing to find substantial amounts of gold, the admiral continued his journey, passing Punta Grande and arriving at a point, which he called Bastimentos. Columbus returned to Spain in November 1504, poor, sick, and disappointed at his apparent lack of success. Unknowingly, however, he had set into motion events of great importance for the isthmus of Panama and Spain. The two places he named Portobelo and Bastimentos (later called Nombre de Dios) were to exercise a seminal role in the development of Afro-colonial culture. By the same token, the founding of Panama la Vieja (The Old City of Panama) and subsequent growth of trade between the Pacific and Atlantic by means of the Camino Real (Royal Road) and the Chagres River were also influential in the growth of Afro-Colonial culture.

To Pedro Arias de Avila fell the honor of capturing Isla del Rey and establishing Panama as a Spanish city on August 15, 1519. "He decided to establish a city that would serve as a point of departure for the explorations that would be made along the coast of the South Sea (Pacific Ocean)" (Carles 1969: 8). Indigenous groups that inhabited the sites that became major Spanish cities—and centers of Afro-Colonial settlement—were conquered, subjugated, and finally forced to flee to the most remote areas of the jungle and mountain ranges. Still, miscegenation among Spaniards, Indians, and Negroes began early in all areas, creating the racial mixtures characteristic of the isthmus today.

Although the exact beginnings of slavery in Panama are uncertain, we find several definitive early references to the introduction of slaves: "In 1500 Ovando received permission to carry thither [to Hispaniola] Negro slaves who had been born under Christian powers" (Browning 1930: 8). Thus, Ferdinand authorized the use of the vast number of slaves who had lived in Seville since the mid-fifteenth century. These slaves (*ladinos*), as well as those who were subsequently brought directly from Africa (*bozales*), were provided by the Portuguese, who dominated the slave trade for some time. The voyage taken by Ojeda and Nicuesa in 1509, designed to colonize Castilla de Oro (early name for Panama) and Veraguas, also brought forty slaves on authority of King Ferdinand (Fortune 1967a: 64).

Despite fears of revolt and paganism, Charles I "granted a patent to one of his Flemish favorites containing an exclusive right to supply 4,000 Negroes annually to Hispaniola, Cuba, Jamaica, and Porto Rico.[2] The favorite sold his patent for 25,000 ducats to some Genovese merchants who obtained the slaves from the Portuguese" (Browning 1930: 9). These same merchants are responsible for the construction of *La Casa de los Genoveses*, a stone house which was the center of the slave trade in the Old City of Panama. Its ruins may be seen today in Panama la Vieja.

Importation of slaves into Panama assumed such proportions early in the sixteenth century that soon the white element of the colonial population was greatly outnumbered. With the rise in importance of Nombre de Dios and later Portobelo, mostly due to the commercial fairs held there and the massing of the gold fleet, the number of slaves and free Negroes rose sharply all along the Camino Real. Small settlements on the royal road, such as Las Cruces, Venta de Chagres, Gorgona, and Matachín, were almost totally populated by Negroes.

There are few population statistics available for the sixteenth century; however, in 1607,[3] a very detailed report was sent to the Council of the Indies in Seville, which listed not only the numbers of slaves, their occupations and sex, but also the civil and domestic status of the entire population. The precision with which the information is presented leads one to place some degree of credence in the figures. The report reveals that even at this relatively early juncture in the history of Panama, there were some free Negroes (*negros horros*) and a fairly complicated system for classifying members of the racially mixed population.

The social structure of the city in 1607 consisted of Spaniards (*vezinos* or *vezinas*), religious orders, *mulatos* and *mulatas* (the product of Spanish and Negro miscegenation), *mestizas* (the result of the union of Spanish and Indian blood), *criollos* (persons born of Spanish blood in the New World), *cuarterones* (the result of the union of a mulata and a Spaniard), *zambaigo* (the racial mixture of Indian and Negro), Indians, and those simply classified as "Negro." The appellation of "slave" was applied to many of the classes above, as well as their offspring. At the same time, evidence shows Negros (*mulatos, quarteroons, horros*), *mestizos*,and Indians also owned slaves.

In spite of many deaths, there seemed to have been a steady and significant growth of the slave community over the years. Within the Negro population, however, the number of free men increased dramatically. By 1778, whereas the slave population in Panama consisted of 1,539 men and 1,254 women for a total of 2,793 people, there were 19,696 free Negroes—9,163 men and 10,533 women (Suarez 1971: 88).

From the beginning of the sixteenth century, Negroes took up residence in bands that made their homes in the jungles of the isthmus. These fugitives (*cimarrones*) and their activities constitute an important chapter in the history of Panama, for the *Cimarrones* are one of the main sources of the Congo tradition which is a focus of the essay.

The Congo tradition is a major Afro-Hispanic folkloric tradition in Panama and is characterized by a Royal Court headed by a king and queen and composed of court members of many types who fulfill diverse functions. They utilize a special dialect in addition to Spanish, and during carnival season present *congadas* (musical dance/theatre), thematic materials and characters from the oral history of slavery during the colonial period.

SOCIOCULTURAL CONTEXT OF
MUSICAL PERFORMANCE

During centuries of adaptation, assimilation, and acculturation, peoples of African descent in Panama have shared much of their culture with the general population. In fact, it may be postulated that many important aspects of expressive culture within the Republic owe their life's blood and substance to Afro-Panamanian heritage. One has only to listen to the drum accompaniment to the national dance, *El Tamborito*. The strong rhythmic style and body movements, characteristic of west African dance, form the substance of Congo music as well as the related styles that are found in towns such as Tucutí and Garachiné.

The contexts in which Afro-Panamanians make music are many and varied. Often the situational context, the time, place, or particulars of a specific event do not vary much from those of other groups. It is in the sociocultural context—the province of the underlying aesthetic—that we reach the heart of the people and their traditions. While the relationship between context and content is not always easy to discern, there are signals and cues which lead us to appreciate the richness and subtlety of such interaction.

The most widespread public feasts are tied to the veneration of Catholic Saints. Once each year, most towns hold a celebration in honor of their patron saint. This saint is considered the protector of the town and typically the church is dedicated to him or the town is named for him.

The town of Portobelo, perhaps the most famous of Afro-Colonial strongholds, has a parish church that dates back to the late seventeenth century (although some sections have been added over the years). Named San Felipe (Saint Phillip), it contains simple wooden benches, alabaster holy water basins, and an ornately painted wooden altar; the tomb of a Spanish viceroy is buried in the floor. The most striking feature of San Felipe, however, is a carved wooden case with a glass front, located high up to the left of the main altar. It houses the much revered statue of *El Cristo Negro* (the Black Christ).

The order of events and duration of the celebrations vary from town to town, but in all cases there is a juxtaposition of the sacred and the profane which recalls a medieval fair.

The religious portion of the Patron Saint Festival begins with a series of masses, novenas, held each night for nine days prior to the Saint's day. Following the novenas, the saint is carried through the principal streets supported on a platform . . . decorated with flowers and lights. Behind the statue devotees from the parish walk in orderly file carrying lighted candles. (Cheville 1977: 22).

While religious activities are going on in the church and street processions are being organized, some town residents are drinking in cantinas, gambling, enjoying other amusements, or preparing for the evening's dances. The event helps to draw the urban and rural sectors together since people who live in the capital, Panama City, Colon, and other larger cities often travel to their native towns for these festivals. It strengthens their sense of identity.

In Portobelo, residents prepare for their feast of the Nazarene for weeks prior to the actual day of celebration, which is October 21. On the days that precede the procession, the locus of activity is the church and its environs. A citizen's committee is in charge of collecting monies and gifts for the saint, decorating the platform on which the statue is to be carried, and dressing El Cristo Negro in his purple robe. Men from the town and other cities come to carry the statue through two small dirt-covered streets. A priest, who typically journeys from Colon to celebrate mass and minister to the community's religious needs, blesses items the people wish to present to the saint. The priest does not participate in the actual procession and veneration, because it is not an official church holy observance.

Even though, in practice, the official Panamanian church hierarchy seems to support the celebration of El Cristo Negro, the festival itself is not really a part of the liturgical calendar. The Passion of Jesus occurs in the dry months, not in October during the rainy season. Thus, the festival is more a folkloric event.

During the feat of El Nazareno, both sacred and secular music play a part. Within the church context are the hymns that are sung during the mass, the dressing of the statue, and decorating of the platform with candles and flowers. Outside the church, one hears small ensembles of accordions and drums, men singing *décimas*, and others playing music for dancing.

The nighttime religious processional proceeds to the cadence of a large bass drum, which marks a slow and steady beat. A small band of brass instruments, and a clarinet or two complete the ensemble. Somber tunes, usually in a minor mode, are repeated frequently as the procession advances, the lighted platform being carried by at least forty men who chant in unison, "Viva El Nazareno! Viva El Cristo Negro!" When the procession begins to make its way through the streets, all other activity ceases and attention is concentrated upon the event at hand.

On Isla del Rey, the tiny hilly town of San Miguel celebrates its patron Saint Michael with "devil dances." "Los Gran Diablos," as they are called in the central provinces, appear as *Los Diablos de Los Espejos* (The Mirror Devils). Elaborately dressed in masks, long-tiered hats with colored cloth streamers, and hooped multicolored skirts with mirrors adorning their sashes, the devils dramatically reenact Lucifer's battle with the forces of good. Poetic texts and intricate dance choreography characterize this celebration. (Mirror devils are also preserved in the traditions of La Chorrera, Portobelo, and Garachiné.)

There are no rules or set structures for the celebration of these local festivals. Each town and city may celebrate either the founding, the birthday of a famous native son, an historical event of importance or an agricultural event. During this time, the sacred/profane continuum is continually travelled as both religious and secular activities intertwine. This is important for it illustrates how a multiplicity of community needs are met within the context of a communal celebration.

Despite the flexibility of structure, there are elements that seem to be a part of local feasts: cock fights, bull fights, horse races, street processions, and both social and traditional folk dances. Traditional costumes are very much in evidence at these times as are folk instruments and singing. Accompanying all these activities are fairs, where handicrafts are made and sold to the general public. Hats and bags for carrying all sorts of possessions are favorite items. Food and drink are sold in stalls that line the streets, completing the complex mosaic that pulsates through the small towns and cities that dot the interior of the country.

The one social event that captures the most people is the carnival. Each year, the entire population of Panama prepares for the final four days that precede the onset of Lent. In Congo tradition, preparations and dancing begin as early as the twentieth of January. In all areas of the country, groups make costumes, practice songs and dances, and *comparsas* (street ensembles who sing and play during the festivities) rehearse. Carnival has always been a special time for those on the lower rungs of the social ladder, for it is traditionally a time when the strata of society may be overturned.

THE NATURE OF AFRO-PANAMANIAN MUSICAL STYLE: BUILDING BLOCKS

Of course, the building blocks of Afro-Panamanian music are not completely different in kind from those of other musics performed in the country. The differences lie in degree and style of performance. I would like to concentrate on the dynamic interaction of Afro-Panamanian music, singers, instrumentalists, and dancers.

While relatively few musical instruments are actively used within the tradition, this does not preclude diversity of musical expression nor dynamic performance. Instruments form only a part of the ensemble. When combined with a chorus of female singers and a soloist, the result is a musical composition of great force and inventiveness.

MUSICAL INSTRUMENTS

The traditional music of Panama incorporates instruments from all categories in the Sachs/Hornbostel classification, with the exception of the electrophone. Transverse wooden flutes, conch horns, bone flutes, *güiros*, stamping tubes, guitars, violins, *mejoranas*, accordions, and several kinds of drums are used as solo instruments and in varying ensembles. With such great instrumental variety available, it is indeed interesting that Afro-Panamanian traditions predominately employ membranophones.

Drums, along with singing and hand-clapping, make up the orchestra for the "Baile de Tambor." (drum dance).[4] As in much of West Africa, the Afro-Panamanian musical aesthetic is based on an ever-present percussive quality. Even when voices are employed percussive effects are an important feature of the style. Drums not only enhance the percussive texture of the singers' voices and hands but also add to the complexity as they introduce several other rhythmic patterns which, in turn, may vary during a composition.

While generally in the Panamanian musical tradition, there seems to be no magic or special status ascribed to drums or the persons who play them, some degree of reverence is accorded the instrument when it is being played. During a *baile de tambor*, dancers perform several special steps and movements before the drum. El *Tamborito*, the national dance of Panama, has a special segment called *los tres golpes* (the three strokes) in which the dancers (male and female) step before the drums in a form of salute. At a signal, they rhythmically move three steps backward; then, they begin the choreography, which constitutes the dance proper. In most Afro-Panamanian areas, dancers salute the drum ensemble before they begin the dance proper; however, their subsequent choreography is more flexible.

The Queen of the Congos of Colón, Lilia Perea, once told me that the drummers could refuse to play for someone, such as an intruder to the group. In this case, they throw the drums to the ground. Then the intruder must pay for the honor of listening and dancing to the drums or else leave the dancing area.

The only significant study of the drum in Panama has been done by the late folklorist, Manuel F. Zárate (1962; 1963). His observations, coupled with my own and those of Raymond L. George, a former staff member of the National Museum of Panama, provide the data for the discussion that follows on the Panamanian drum.

Some drums are most definitely of West Central African origin. Zárate (1963: 6) always strong in his denial of significant African influence on the folklore of Panama, had to acknowledge that "each one of the types that came to America [European and African drums] have conserved their original characteristics with little or no variation." Congo traditions and related musical styles, notably those of the people of San Miguel and the Darién, seem to be the most outstanding cases of African influence in Panama. African influence upon other groups in such practices as singing and dancing is much harder to ascertain. It appears to me that through the centuries, the general culture has absorbed so much African culture that the people no longer view its traditions as foreign.[5]

There are two distinct prototypes of drums used in the folk music of Panama. "One is single-headed and open ended which is played with the hands, which we call *tambor*; the other is double-headed and closed, which is played with sticks, which we call *caja*" (Zárate 1963: 6). The *tambora* variety is usually found among peoples of African heritage, though San Miguel inhabitants, who are descendants of slaves and Indians, use the *redoblante* variety. (Their drum is somewhat larger than most *redoblantes*, however, being more like an orchestral bass drum.) It is important to note that often the mere availability of an instrument influences its choice, not only underlying aesthetic norms. The *tambor*[6] comes in four shapes (see figure 10.2). Certain forms are usually more common in the mestizo areas of the country, while others seem to be more characteristic of Panamanians of African descent. Although I present all of the forms here for the sake of comparison, I will discuss in depth only the materials, methods of construction, playing style, and cultural diffusion of the instruments used by the Congos and related groups. In many instances, the materials and methods of construction are the same, while the playing style and diffusion are typically what varies.

All the *tambores* of Panama are made from a single section of a tree trunk and have cylindrical or conical bores. The actual pitch of the drum will depend more upon the diameter of the head, internal bore, and the tension of the skin than on the actual length of the drum body. The earlike projections on each *tambor* (see figure 10.2) are wedges (*cuñas*), which are used to increase the tension

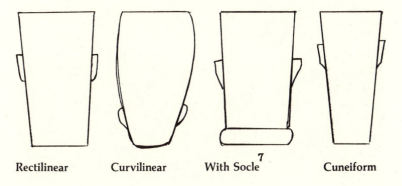

Rectilinear   Curvilinear   With Socle[7]   Cuneiform

Figure 10.2 Common shapes of the *tambor* of Panama

upon the heads. They are primarily a tuning device. The *caja*, a cylindrical drum, has two versions: the larger one, sometimes called *caja tambora*, has laced heads, which are tuned by tightening the cords connecting them; the other, called *caja redoblante*, has a wooden rim fastened over the head and is tuned by adjusting the tension on the rim. It resembles a European field drum.

The materials from which drums are made can be found in or near any town of the Panamanian interior. Zárate (1962: 48) gives a very detailed list of the woods used, along with their relative suitability for drum making:

The woods are chosen in accord with the quality of sound that is desired, with the possibilities of the region and tools at your disposal. The most common for *tambores*, in order of quality are: cedar, el "indio," el corotú, balsa, coconut palm, and el "volador." For the *cajas* cedar and corotú are always used. To hold the skin over the opening, a strong vine (*bejuco*) is wrapped on the ends. The strings or cords for tuning are of manila, sisal, abacá, wool, and though rarely, of strips of the same hide which is twisted.[7]

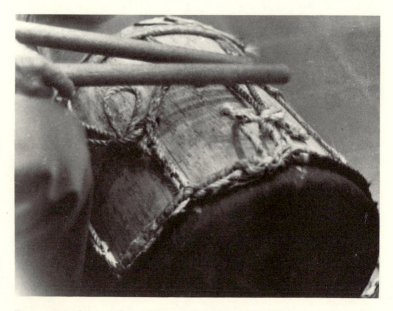

Figure 10.3 Caja tambora, Tucutí, Province of Darién

In actuality, the choice of wood really does not seem to make much difference. Most of the woods used are relatively soft—the balsa being the softest—and can be worked by means of the machete and chisel. The sound produced by any drum is more dependent on the diameter of the head and the type of skin as well as the amount of tension on the head. At the same time, however, various types of wood offer such advantages as resistance to insects, moisture, cracking, and weathering.[8]

The construction of the drums is done by individuals in the towns of the interior or the members of the various performing groups. Before the drum maker can begin to carve, the wood must be somewhat dry. He can then carve the outside and clear the inner bore with his long-handled chisel. The major cutting work is performed with a machete. Once the drum has been cut and shaped, it must then be dried again—preferably in the shade —before the head can be put on. If the drying process is not completed properly, the drum could develop cracks and eventually split. Once the body has been prepared, and the mouth smoothed to receive the head, the skin is cut to the desired diameter (having previously been cleaned of all hair), placed on the ring of rattan vine (*bejuco*), and then mounted upon the drum.

The skins used for drum heads come from several kinds of animals. The primary choice is the skin of deer, with goat, *saino* (a type of wild pig), and various types of wild cats following in order of preference.

There are many methods used to cleanse the skin of hair. Zárate (1962: 49) describes one process: "Before the final softening carefully remove the hair with a knife or as a more sure method, with a rough stone or brick, until the skin is very smooth."

Informants have told me that they take ashes from a fire and rub them into the hair. After letting the skin stand awhile, they rub it with a sharp knife to remove the loosened hair.

Following the cleaning, the skin is soaked in water to make it pliable. It is then applied to the ring of *bejuco* and doubled over. Holes are made in the skin close to the ring of *bejuco* and cords are strung through them. These cords will later be connected to a waistband of sorts, which circles the drum body. On curvilinear drums of the *mestizo* areas, the waistband is located more toward the bottom of the body, while in the rectilinear and cuneiform drums (both with and without the *socle*), the waistband is found very near the retaining ring of vine. Wedges (*cuñas*) are placed between the drum body and the waistband. Through the application of force on the *cuñas*, usually achieved by pounding with a hammer or other heavy object, the head is pulled downward at the edges and thus tightened. The increased tension tunes the drum head to a higher pitch. Zárate (1962: 49) reports that at this point "the tambor is placed in the sun to cure it for several hours each day, and then finally tuned to the point that the expert considers it has achieved the quality of sound desired."

Drums are typically not varnished or painted when completed, although the Congos of Colón have painted their drums with silver and black paint and in some *mestizo* areas I have seen them painted green or brown. One drum (Congo) is even named and dated: *El Nuevo Relámpago* 1970 (The New Lightning 1970). This is a common practice in the Yalemba area of old Belgium Congo (Zaire).

Although there may be minor variations in the materials of construction, or the procedures, the basic method of construction is always the same. Of the drum shapes which are shown in figure 10.2, the rectilinear form is most often made by Congo drum makers. Some drums approach the cuneiform type; however, it is very difficult at times to decide whether these are two different shapes or variations of the same basic form. The angle of the sides, at times, almost appears to be so slight that the drum could also be considered cylindrical. The drum form which exhibits a *socle* is characteristic of groups from the Darién (Tucutí and Garachiné). The plinth may be straight or flared, as in the base of a mortar. Drums in this form also vary in size and may be quite thin in diameter. As I mentioned in connection with the choice of wood, the head and the tension as well as inner bore and body length contribute more to sound quality than the shape. These aspects might well be the same in two drums of completely different outer form.

The construction process for the *caja* (*tambora*) is not very different from that for the *tambor*, however, Zárate (1962: 49) mentions that with the *tambora*

the heads are attached to the opening by means of a ring of willow twig, the edges are doubled over the ring, and the tuning cords are joined in the form of a "V," with these attaching one head to the other. When the drum has been covered, the heads are tuned moderately and the skins are cleaned of hair.

Drum measurements do not vary greatly throughout the Panamanian regions, but various names designate certain size *tambors*, which are relegated to specific positions within the drum choir. For example, the drum ensemble in the *mestizo* areas—Las Tablas in the province of Los Santos being the Center—comprises three drums: *repicador*, *pujador*, and the *caja* (*redoblante*). The ensembles of the mulatto areas—La Chorrera in the province of Panama and the small towns, such as Antón and Penonomé in the province of Coclé—all consist of four drums, though the basic combinations vary. (See figures 10.4, 10.5, 10.6). The ensemble of Chorrera, for instance, includes the *sequero* (*seco*), the *Claro, pujador* (*pujo*), and the *caja* (*tambora*). There is also a larger *caja*, called the *cumbiero*.[9] It is always used in a stationary position, never carried through the streets as the other drums are.

The Darién—the jungle area adjacent to the Chocó region of Colombia and the home of a good part of the Hispanic Negro population and some Indian tribes—also boasts a drum ensemble of four instruments: *repicador*, *pujador*, *jondo* (*hondo*), and the *caja* (*tambora*) which, in this region, is a barrel shaped drum. (See figure 10.7).

Finally, the congo ensembly provides us with still other names and there are several variations within the tradition itself. As Zárate, and Leslie Raymond George[10] report, the congo choir consists of: *jondo* (*hondo*), *seco*, and a *caja* (*tambora*). One *tambor* is represented twice in the ensemble. Neither Zárate nor George mentions which *tambor* that is, but one of my major informants, Melba de Ardines,[11] asserts that the battery of tambores consists of two *llanos*, one *jondo* (*hondo*), and the *caja* (tambora). While at first thought, listing these drum names may seen unnecessary, they are, in fact, important because they reveal to us something about the underlying aesthetic and function of the drums within the ensemble. Table 10.1 lists the drums in the four geographic areas; each set of drums is presented in order of relative pitch, going from high to low. The *caja* is not part of this schema since it plays a rhythmic role in the ensemble. Notice that, as a rule, there are two

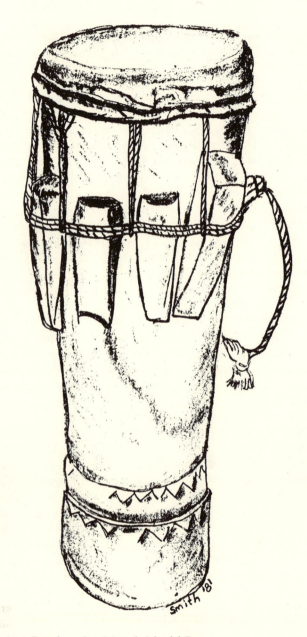

Figure 10.4 Pujador—San Miguel, Isla del Rey

Figure 10.5 *Tambor*—La Chorrera, Province of Panama, Gran Diablos

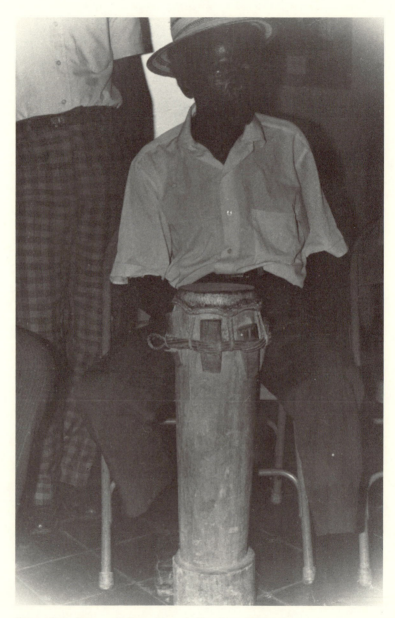

Figure 10.6 Drummer from Tucutí, Province of Darién

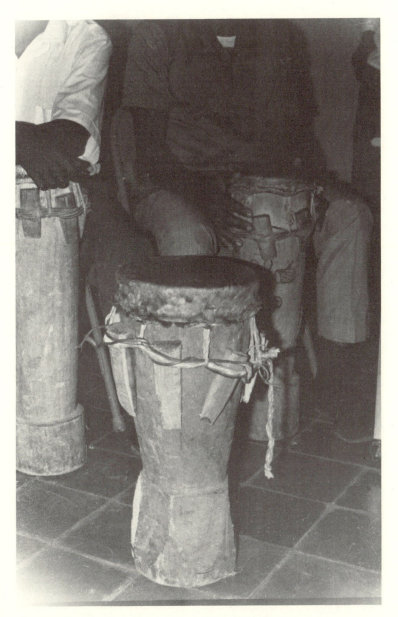

Figure 10.7 Drum ensemble, Tucutí, Province of Darién

or three levels of relative pitch. Uusally, a high drum functions as
the "master" drum. The master drummer improvises and induces
the dancers to change their movement. In ensembles of three
tambores, a medium-voiced drum is assigned basic patterns, which
may vary to some degree. It, too, may give cues to dancers. The
low-voiced drum typically plays basic patterns as well. The names
of the drums often give us an idea as to their intended use within
the particular ensemble—for example, *llamador* (caller), *repicador*
(chimer/pealer), *jondo* (low), and *claro* (high).

In West African drum choirs, often the large drum with the deep
voice is considered to be male and the most important of the ensemble,
providing us with a clue to the African aesthetic. This is
precisely the case in the Atumpan and the Frontonfrom ensemble of
the Ashanti of Ghana.

Table 10.1
Organization of Drum Ensembles in
Representative Geographical Areas

	Las Tablas	Antón/Penonomé
High	Repicador (Chimer/pealer)	Repicador
Medium	X	Llamador (caller)
Low	Pujador (pusher) Caja (R)[a]	Pujador Caja (T)[b]

	Chorrera	Darien
High	Sequero (Seco)	Repicador
Medium	Claro	Pujador
Low	Pujador Caja (T)	Jondo Caja (T)

[a]Caja *redoblante.*
[b]Caja *tambora.*

The ensemble as described by Ardines (1973) functions in this way: "The jondo (hondo) is largest and the llano smallest. The caja calls, the jondo answers and the rest follow. If the caja does not play, the drums cannot follow. They can play without the caja but it does not result as well as when they use it." It is apparent that in her conception of the ensemble, the *caja* plays the same role that the bell or gong does in a West African percussion ensemble— maintaining the meter/pattern and tempo. This allows the *hondo*, the deep and important voice, to lead the other *tambores*. George (1972) reports that one of the major drummers from the same group of Congos in Colón relayed to him that the *hondo* is an important voice in his ensemble, but it is now the highest pitch drum; it functions as the *repicador*. This shift is indicative of the Congo penchant for improvisation. As you will recall from previous discussion, the pitch of the drum is changed by varying the tension on the heads and striking the drum in a certain place.[12]

It should be noted that the people of the Congo tradition do not often use these individual drum names. The Congo aesthetic requires that one frequently call an object by a name that is opposite to the generally accepted one. Thus, Congo members call their drums, "violín." The drummers are also called by a special name: *Gallineta* (woodcock).

Table 10.2
Congo Drum Ensemble

	A	B
High	Jondo (hondo)	Llano (two)
Low	Seco	Jondo (hondo)
	Caja (T)	Caja (T)

DRUM SIZE

There is only slight variance among the drum sizes in the *mestizo*, mulatto, and Congo groups. (See table 10.3 for measurements of various *tambores* and *caja*.)

Table 10.3
Comparative Drum Measurements
(Given in centimeters: 2.5 cm = 1 inch)

	Height	Upper Diameter
Las Tablas		
Pujador	54	23
Repicador	50	20
Caja	17	27
La Chorrera		
Pujador	61	23
Claro	49	21
Sequero	53	15
Caja	42	45
Cumbiero	52	28
(Zárate 1962: 47)		
Los Congos of Colón		
Jondo	51	19
Seco	53	22
Caja	36	25
(George 1972: 5)		
Los Congos of Portobelo		
Seco	55	25
Jondo	54	23
(requinto)		

(No caja was mentioned in this reference.)

	Lower Diameter	Thickness
Las Tablas		
Pujador	15	3
Repicador	14	3
Caja		2.5
La Chorrera		
Pujador	17	4
Claro	19	6
Sequero	13	2
Caja	42	2
Cumbiero	19	4.5
(Zárate 1962: 47)		

Table 10.3 (continued)

	Lower Diameter	Thickness
Los Congos of Colón		
Jondo	17	X
Seco	18	X
Caja		
(George 1972: 5)		
Los Congos of Portobelo		
Seco	23	X
Jondo	19	X
(requinto)		
(No caja was mentioned in this reference.)		
(George 1972: 2)		

In general, the drums in the town of Chorrera are the largest in Panama. The *caja tambora* is always larger than the *caja redoblante*. In the Darién area, the *caja* may be of a greater size because barrels are used for the body of the instrument. Only among the ensembles of Tucutí, Garachiné (in the province of Darién), and San Miguel on Isla del Rey in the archipelago of Las Perlas have I ever seen a Panamanian drum with the *socle* at the bottom.

To play the *tambores*, a performer usually sits with the *tambor* tightly pressed between his lower legs. He strikes the *tambor* with his bare hands and, at times, raises and lowers the drum body with his knees, so as to use the ground beneath the drum in his quest for tonal variation. He also strikes the head of the *tambor* at various points with his fingers and butt of his hands to produce different tonal effects. During a procession through the streets of a town, the performer suspends the *tambor* from his neck, using a rope strap. The strap is long enough so that the drummer can play the drum with both hands either in front of him or slightly to the side.

The *caja* is also played in a sitting position; however, technique differs. The performer always uses two wooden sticks to strike the head of the *caja*. While one stroke is always on the drum head, sometimes the performer also strikes the body of the instrument. Although this drum has two membranes, only one is used during performance.

188   Ronald R. Smith

Among the people of Tucutí, rather than place the drum between his legs, the drummer puts the *caja* on the floor or ground and holds it in place with one foot as he plays. The Congo tradition demonstrates a somewhat different technique in that the performer holds the instrument on his thigh (while he is seated) and plays on the head that faces forward. In this position, it is difficult to play on the sides; however, the performer can play on the edge (usually called the "rim," although the *caja tambora* has no rim as such). In San Miguel, the *caja*'s large size makes it unnecessary for the drummer to use his foot to stabilize it. During processions, the *caja* is suspended from a strap, as are all of the drums, and played with the sticks striking one head. The sticks may vary in size and diameter; they are not necessarily manufactured for the purpose of playing the *caja*. (See figure 10.8 which shows characteristic rhythms of an ensemble in the Congo tradition.)

Figure 10.8 Drums, Tucutí, Province of Darién

OTHER INSTRUMENTS IN THE ENSEMBLES

Although Afro-Panamanians most frequently use drums, a few other instruments deserve our attention. The accordion, guitar, violin, shaker, and mortar (*almiréz*) do perform specific roles in ensembles and we can best examine their salient characteristics by looking at the ensembles in which they are found.

As we have seen, in Congo tradition, long practiced along the Caribbean coast (see figure 10.1, nos. 10, 9, 8, 7, 3, 2, and 4) and in the capital city of Panama, drums comprise the complete ensembles. The same is true in Tucutí (not shown in figure 10.1 but located some thirty miles to the east of Garachiné, (no. 12), La Chorrera (no. 1), and Chepo (no. 13). Antón (no. 5), however, preserves a unique ensemble in which, together with male drummers, a woman performs on a small metal mortar (almiréz). This instrument, more characteristically found in an apothecary's shop or used in a kitchen to crush condiments such as garlic, is held in one hand and struck inside with a small metal rod, held by the other. The resulting pulse is equidistant, fast, and without accent. It constitutes the smallest unit of pulsation and seems to function as an orientation device for other members of the ensemble. In no other group do we find this sort of rhythmic device.

The ensemble which accompanies the mirror devils (Diablos de Los Espejos) of Garchiné (see no. 12) is also distinctive in that it contains only one drum and an accordion. This drum is mortar type (flared socle) and has a single head; however, it is not played In the same manner as similar drums in Tucutí. The performer uses only one stick to strike the head and rim of the drum, playing a series of simple rhythmic patterns in accompaniment to the accordion's short melodic phrases.

San Miguel (see no. 11) perhaps displays the most variety in terms of instruments. In addition to two pujadors and a caja, it is not uncommon to find a violin and guitar, though the latter do not necessarily play at the same time. Completing the ensemble is a hand-held metal tube about twelve to fifteen inches long, containing seeds or stones. Shaken by the performer, it functions somewhat as the mortar in Antón—orienting other members of the ensemble. Figure 10.8 illustrates the relationship of drums in a Congo ensemble . The designations Atravesao (6 + 8) and Terrible (2 + 4) are used by members of this tradition to differ metric organizations. (See figure 10.9)

SINGERS AND SINGING

The simple materials used to construct instruments do not preclude a wide variety of songs. Nevertheless, the variety of media

Figure 10.9 Characteristic Congo drum patterns: "Atravesao"—Terrible

used to achieve musical expression is somewhat limited. Two basic
groups—singers and instrumentalists—manipulate the resources
available.

The vocal group, always composed of women, includes a leader
(*cantalante*) and a chorus (*segundas*). In Congo tradition, these
women would be members of the Queen's court. In any other setting, they would be assembled from the resident population. Upon
these women rests much of the responsibility for animating a performance. They freely move out of the chorus to dance in the dance

area, returning when they are replaced by other female dancers. The energy and excitement generated by their hand-clapping and singing is a major component of *bailes de tambor*. Singing style is very uniform from group to group, with the greatest variation occurring in the vocal ability and stamina of the individual leaders (*cantalantes*). One immediately notices that the overriding aspect of vocal style is the *forte*. There is almost no relief from this dynamic level of sound, whether during a specific composition or at some point during the performance. Vocal stamina is considered a desirable attribute in a *cantalante*. She must be able to perform for extended periods of time (a *congada*—a musical event, during which *Congo* groups dance, sing, and enact mimetic drama episodes—may last all night or at least several hours), as well as project both her melodic material and her text over the chorus and instruments. The *segundas* may number ten or more women, while the instrumental ensemble consists of four drums. Extraneous noises whether from spectators or from elsewhere, also provide competition for the leader. From the moment she sets the tonality of a selection and its beginning tempo, she throws her voice forward with unflagging energy, continuing in this manner until the end of the composition.

The *segundas* must also have a good deal of stamina, although their role is not as demanding as the leader's, for they, too, sing during the entire event. The dynamic level of the answering refrain, which they sing, is also very high; however, the larger number of voices permits each individual to conserve more energy than the leader can. The special sound of the Panamanian woman's voice is not, however, produced solely through loud singing. Use of the upper range of the voice, no vibrato, and extreme tension produce a timbre that can best be described as strident and penetrating.

Using the voice in this manner does not often permit such vocal coloring or subtle musical effects. Nevertheless, combining this penetrating vocal quality with rhythmic syncopations and percussive effects in the vocal line generates excitement and musical interest. Vocal ornamentation is not particularly important. There are, however, a few ornaments, such as small, falling melodic motifs at the ends of phrases, vocables with no semantic meaning, and a variety of exclamations, which are merely vehicles for expressing excitement.

DANCE

In Panama, dance seems to be the most sensational way of expressing the nonverbal aspects of the aesthetic. It almost seems as if dance is the common denominator, since songs end in dance— that is, they always stimulate someone to begin dancing—and drumming finds a subtle interpretation in the translation to body movement.

In Panamanian tradition, dance can sometimes be thoroughly integrated with theater and song; at other times, it is somewhat independent. Whether it functions in one manner or the other, it still possesses its own particular characteristics and aesthetic.

In terms of choreography, Afro-Panamanian dance is very simple, for there is no rigidly established floor plan. Its complexity arises rather from the confluence of body movements and variation in male and female styles.

In addition to programmatic aspects of dance and variation of meter among Congos, we can ascertain characteristic movement styles for men and women. The two distinct styles complement each other at all points during their interaction. The *Baile de Tambor* is a couple dance, which is free enough in its protocol to allow new partners to enter the dancing area at will, be they men or women. But there are never more than two dancers in the area at one time, except during the *cumbia*, a group circle dance.

During celebrations, participants may dance for extended periods. Despite the constant vigorous movement and activity, we find young children, middle-aged persons, grandmothers and grandfathers, and even pregnant women near their delivery dates participating. There is no special choreography for little girls or young boys; each may dance with adult members of the opposite sex and must learn to make the kinds of movements that their sex role demands.

As is the case for the *cantalante,* the drummers, the dancers, and individuals improvise and often develop a personal style which they practice within the boundaries of the general tradition. The freedom to show some degree of dexterity and personal expression has prompted some dancers to develop movements that not only identify them, but draw the viewers into a greater appreciation of the dance as they recognize their favorite dancers. Thus, individual personality is allowed to flower, though within the limits of the characteristic style.

In a *congada* the King and Queen are traditionally the first to dance. The monarchs and subsequent dancers all perform an act of reverence in front of the drums before they begin the dance proper. As discussed earlier, the national dance of Panama, *el tamborito*, also incorporates a similar feature called *los tres golpes*, where the dancers step in place until one of the drums plays a high, fast roll (*repica*) and then take three synchronized steps backward, which end in a quick turn. The dancers are now face to face and thus begin the *vuelta* (turn) or *sequidilla* section of the dance. The *tres golpes* section follows the *paseo* of the couple, which takes them around the circle—one on either side—in counterclockwise motion. These stylized dance movements are, in themselves, a salute to the drums.

The Congos, on the other hand, may begin with a salute to the drums, with the dance following. At times, when the Queen dances, she may take her partner's hand and step in place before the drum; the woman smoothly swings her *pollera* (large, flaring skirt) in a back-and-forth motion, almost as if she had wings. When the main drum signals with a *repica*, the woman turns smoothly and quickly, as if on wheels, and begins to move around the ring or square. Cheville (1977) and Zárate (1963) have called the dance of the Congo a "primitive" form of the *tamborito*.

The dance is one of courtship, though the relationship is never consummated. The attitude assumed by the man is one of pursuit, while the woman is, at times, seductive, arrogant, aggressive, and elusive. Most of the activity takes place in front of or near the drums, depending on the size of the dancing area. During the constant pursuit and woman's rejection of the man, the couple do not usually touch; rather, they inscribe many circles and turns with their bodies. Contact results only at those moments when the man attempts to kiss or touch the woman and she rapidly turns and bumps him with the side or back of her hip. Most often, she is successful in evading him completely. The whole tone of the dance is somewhat erotic, the mood accentuated by the predominant utilization of pelvic movements by both the man and the woman. The most intense interaction is maintained by means of eye contact. Although the woman may often lose sight of the man momentarily as she makes her evasive movements, she remains the focal point of his attention and activity. Both partners' evasive movements and turns are executed with such rapidity and smoothness that it often seems that they knew beforehand what was going to happen. The woman always seems to know where the man is, even when she has given him her back for the moment. Here, the members' familiarity with personal styles of the others in their group often helps the dancers in pursuit and evasion.

The dominant mood of the woman's style is one of control and self-assurance. She holds her head erect and slightly to the back while maintaining an expression of seductiveness on her face. Some women will only lower their heads and glance at the floor when making a fast turn, holding out to either side the large flaring skirt (*pollera*) and moving it in a wave-like fashion. This causes them to hold their shoulders up and to extend their arms fully. Occasionally, a woman will allow the skirt to fall from her hands and then move her hands from side to side in rhythm.

The locus of important movement during the dance is the pelvic region. The woman attempts to move in such a fashion that almost all her upper body remains still, while she constantly contracts the pelvic area. This gives the impression of a rolling of the stomach and the hips.

The most common foot movement is the *sequidilla* step, a short shuffling step in which both feet remain on the floor, one being pushed forward and the other dragged behind. The distance moved in each step is usually very small, making the woman look as if she is gliding along with a small rocking motion. Combined with pelvic undulations—usually done in tempo with the major subdivisions of the meter—the *sequidilla* step allows the woman to maintain a firm control of her body, to balance, and to present an erotic stance. At times, she poses before the man, as she invites him closer with her eyes and body. At the very moment the man does approach, the woman oftentimes, with a sudden lurch forward eludes him. She avoids his touch—and his advances—by turning away, moving to one side with a great flourish of the skirt. Or she arrogantly faces him and gathers the skirt up in front of her body in a great swoop, thus preventing his "entry." At times, she also becomes very aggressive and actually advances in the man's direction, always moving her pelvis in an undulating fashion, seeming to challenge him to approach.

Since the emphasis is on the relationship of the dancing couple as they advance and retreat, we find that schematic drawings of movement patterns on the floor reveal the circles they inscribe around each other and their sharp diagonal movements to one side or the other. Some individual dancers tend to make greater use of the available dancing space than others. The constant shift from seductiveness to aggressiveness, or vice versa, often causes the dancers to move quickly from one side of the dancing area to the other, only to remain there for a short while in an intense episode.

The man's movements are most often angular and acrobatic. When he approaches the area to begin dancing he often enters with jumping movements, bent at the waist, with arms swinging from side to side. The male dancer's attention is at all times intensely concentrated on the female. At times, he "performs" for her by making many acrobatic movements in front of her. He sometimes also bends close to the floor, his head and face always turned toward the woman, often gazing directly at her pelvic movements as he reciprocally undulates his pelvic region. His legs are usually spread apart for fast jumping movements, though they are moved closer together when he executes the *seguidilla* step. In his attempts to make contact with the woman, the male never uses his hands at any time; he merely lurches forward with his head or his shoulders. His aggressivity is not extreme, as he is always easily eluded; however he is persistent in his pursuit.

Thus, although both dancers use the *sequidilla* step and pelvic undulations, their general styles are distinct. The woman's smooth and flowing movement contrasts sharply with the man's jumpy and angular style. The general stance of the body is also characteristically quite different, with the woman most often erect and elongated in her posture; the man, often stooping and crouching or bent at the waist.

CONCLUSION

Energy, dynamic interaction, the voices of drums, and people come together in Panama for musical experience that, although unique, is very much a part of the larger world of Afro-America. Present research has delineated some of the intricacies of this larger picture, but it remains a task for future investigators to uncover more of the subtleties of performance and the underlying aesthetic.

In Afro-America, the focus is community and extended family. Analysis, therefore, must be at these levels. Communities and their events must be studied in a more holistic manner, for when Afro-Americans sing with the voice of the drum, they sing to their brothers and sisters throughout the hemisphere.

NOTES

1. All quotes and texts originally appearing in Spanish are translated by the author.
2. Permission was granted in 1518 (Carles 1969: 73).
3. See Pineda (1908: 140-175) for details of early census reports.
4. *Baile de tambor* is the term used by Manual Zárate (1962: 1963) to designate the national dance, *tamborito*, and all dances of its general type, that is, courtship or couple dances which are accompanied by drums.
5. Until approximately a generation ago, *La Danza de los Negros Bozales* or *Los Cuenecue* (a dance of newly arrived African people) was performed in the central provinces, the veritable stronghold of *mestizo* folklore. Recently, it has been revived by people in the area.
6. For clarity and consistency, Spanish names will be used in discussing drums.
7. The *indio* and *corotú* are woods like cedar, while the *volador* is a palm.
8. Cedar is "the name applied to a variety of trees . . . most of which are evergreen and have aromatic, often red or red-tinged wood which in many cases is decay-resistant and insect-repellent" (*Encyclopedia Britannica*, Vol. 5, p. 129).
9. Zárate (1962: 54). See figure 10.2 for relative measurements.
10. As reported by Zárate (1962) and George (1972).
11. As reported by Ardines (1973). In this case, one of the *llanos* would function as a medium-voiced drum.
12. "When a round plate vibrates, nodal lines are likely to form concentric circles along some diameters. [Thus] when hit nearer the rim, a drum generally favors higher partials; nearer the center, lower partials. At the point of impact, in any case, the particular overtone corresponding to the nodal division of the point is weakened or eliminated" (Levarie 1968: 151, 155).

REFERENCES

(Works listed include a general bibliography as well as sources cited.

Arce, Enrique, and Juan B. Sosa. 1911. *Compendio de História de Panamá.* Panamá: Edición de la Lotería Nacional de Beneficencia para conmemorar los cien años de la independencia de 1821. (Edición de la 1911: 1971).

Archivo General de Indias, Sevilla, Spain. 1597-1582. "Pacificación de Cimarrones en Tierra Firme." (Mimeograph of a collection of *legajos* in the original Spanish.)

Ardines, Melba. 1973. Interview with author. Colón, Republic of Panama.

Bastide, Roger. 1969. *Las Américas Negras*. Madrid: Alianza Editorial Trans. Patricio Azcárate.

Browning, J. B. 1930. "Negro Companions of the Spanish Explorers in the New World." *Howard University Studies in History*. No. XI, Washington, D.C.

Carles, Ruben D. 1969. *220 Años del Periodo Colonial de Panamá*. Tercera Edición. Panamá: Imprenta Nacional.

Castillero Calvo, Alfredo. 1969. "Los Negros y Mulatos Libres en la História Social Panhameña," *Lotería, Vol. XIV*, No. 163.

Cheville, Lila. 1964. "Folk Dances of Panama." Ph.D. dissertation, University of Iowa.

Cheville, Lila, and Richard. 1977. *Festivals and Dances of Panama*. Panama: Lila and Richard Cheville.

Fortune, Armando. 1967. "Los Primeros Negros en el Istmo de Panamá, por la Libertad," *Lotería* (a) Vol. XII, No. 143; (b) Vol. XII, No. 144.

_____. 1969. "Los Negros cimarrones en Tierra Firme y su Lucha por la Libertad," *Lotería* (a) Vol. XVI, No. 171; (b) Vol. XVI, No. 172; (c) Vol. XVI, No. 173; (d) Vol. XVI, No. 174.

George, Leslie. 1972. Unpublished manuscript, with author.

Guillot, Carlos Federico. n.d. *Negros Rebeldes y Negros Cimarrones* (Perfil afro-americana en la história del nuevo mundo durante el siglo XVI). Buenos Aires: Farina Editores.

Levarie, Siegmund, and Ernest Levy. 1968. *Tone: A Study in Musical Acoustics*. Ohio: Kent State Press.

Pineda, Juan de. (ed.). 1908. *Relaciones Históricas y Geográficas de America Central*. Colección de libros y documentos referentes a la história de América. Tomo VIII. Madrid: Librería General de Victoriano Suarez.

_____. "Descripción de Panamá y su provincia" (sacadad de la relación que por mando del Consejo hizo y embio aquella Audiencia—año 1607) por Don Juan Requejo Salcedo en 1640.

Price, Richard. 1973. *Maroon Societies. Rebel Slave communities in the Americas*. New York: Anchor Press/Doubleday.

Shafroth, John F. 1953. *Panamá La Vieja*. Panamá: Imprenta Nacional.

Smith, Marjorie. 1958. "Progress report on the study of African influences in the music of Panama." *Actas del XXXIII Congreso Internacional de Americanistas*. Vol. II.

Smith, Ronald R. 1976. "The Society of Los Congos of Panama: An Ethno-musicological Study of the Music and Dance-Theater of an Afro-Panamanian Group." Ph.D. dissertation, Indiana University.

Sosa, Juan B. 1919. *Panamá La Vieja.* Panamá: Imprenta Nacional (Con motive del cuatro centenario de su fundación, 1519-1919).

Suarez, Omar Jaen. 1971. "Estadística Demográfica de Panamá: Segunda Mitad del Siglo XVII," *Anales de Ciencias Humanas, Centro de Investigaciones Sociales y Económicas de la Universidad de Panamá,* numiero I, Diciembre.

Torres de Arauz, Reina. 1975. *Darién Panama: Dirección de Patrimonio Histórico,* Instituto Nacional de Cultura.

Webster, Edwin. 1970. *The Defense of Portobelo.* Panama: Florida State University Isthmian Anthropology Society.

Weischoff, Heina. 1933. *Die Afrikanischen Trommeln und Ihre Ausser-afrikanischen Bezeihungen.* Stuttgart: Stecker and Schroder/Verlag.

Zárate, Manuel F. 1958. "Los Congos," *La Estrella de Panamá.* April 17.

_____. 1962. *Tambor y Socavón.* Panamá: Ministerio de Educación, Departamento de Bellas Artes.

_____. 1963. "Tambores de Panama," *Folklore Americano,* año XI-XII, No. 11-12, Lima, Peru, 1963-64.

Index

The Contributors

W. KOMLA AMOAKU, Professor and Chairman of the Department of Music at Central State University in Wilberforce, Ohio, has broad research interests in African and African-American music. He has also published extensively on Orff Schulwerk and traditional African music.

JACQUELINE COGDELL DJEDJE is Assistant Professor in the Department of Music at the University of California, Los Angeles. She has conducted extensive field studies in Afro-American religious music and the West African one-string fiddle traditions. In addition to reviews, articles, and a recording, her publications include *American Black Spiritual and Gospel Songs from Southeast Georgia: A Comparative Study and Distribution of the One-String Fiddle in West Africa.*

NISSIO FIAGBEDZI is a lecturer and acting head of the Department of Music, School of Performing Arts at the University of Ghana. He was a member of the advisory board to the Center for Ethnic Music at Howard University. His publications in the Journal for the Society for Ethno-musicology, *Ethnomusicology*, include "Religious Music Traditions in Africa: A Critical Evaluation of Contemporary Problems and Challenges," "Observations on the Study of African Musical Cultures," and "A Preliminary Inquiry into Inherent Rhythms in Anlo Dance Drumming."

DAPHNE D. HARRISON is Associate Professor and Chairperson of the African American Studies Department at the University of Maryland-Baltimore County. Her principal research efforts have been directed to the contributions of Black women blues singers to American music, and the role of the music in rituals where trance-possession occurs.

MANTLE HOOD is senior Distinguished Professor of Ethnomusicology at the University of Maryland-Baltimore County and was the founder-director of the Institute of Ethnomusicology at UCLA. His specialized interests are on the music of Indonesia, West Africa, and Hawaii. He has published widely in the field of Ethnomusicology; his most recent book (1980) is *Music of the Roaring Sea, Book I* of the trilogy *The Evolution of Javenese Gamelan*.

BENNETTA JULES-ROSETTE is Professor and Chairperson of the Department of Sociology at the University of California, San Diego. She received her Ph.D. (1973) in Social Relations from Harvard University. Since 1969, she has conducted a series of field studies on African religion and art in Southwestern Zaire, Lusaka, Zambia, and most recently Abidjan, Ivory Coast. Her publications include *African Apostles* (1975), *The New Religions in Africa* (1979), *Symbols of Change* (1981), *The Message of Tourist Art* (1984), and numerous articles on African women, art, and culture change.

BRUNO NETTL is Professor of Music and Anthropology at the University of Illinois. He has carried out fieldwork among the Blackfoot Indians, in Iran, and in Israel, and has served as president of the Society for Ethnomusicology and editor of its journal. He has published several books including *Theory and Method in Ethnomusicology* (1964), *Eight Urban Musical Cultures* (1978), and *The Study of Ethnomusicology*.

ROBERT W. NICHOLLS is a Ph.D. student at Howard University. He was born and educated in London and has been a member of the faculty of the Institute of Education, Ahmadu Bello University, Zaria, Nigeria, where he taught Visual Art and Education. He was the secretary of the Action Planning Committee of the Kaduna State Branch of the Nigeria Audio Visual Association (NAVA), a voluntary organization concerned with promoting educational technology within the Nigerian educational system.

RONALD R. SMITH is an Assistant Professor in the Department of Folklore at Indiana University, Bloomington and Director of the Ethnomusicology Program. He previously taught at Bowdoin College (Maine) and Middlebury College (Vermont). He has been a consultant to several departments at the Smithsonian Institution in Washington. He is author of articles on Latin American and Afro-American musics with his principal area of research being Afro-Hispanic music and culture.

DAVID B. WELCH is an Associate Professor of Music in the School of Contemporary Arts at Ramapo College of New Jersey, where he has taught courses in Ethnomusicology and Musical Theatre since 1972. He has published articles on Yoruba traditional music and West African musical retentions in Haiti and Bahia, Brazil, in *Revue D'Histoire du Theatre* and the *Yearbook of the International Folk Music Council*. He has contributed to the Festschrift for Klaus Wachsmann, *Essays for a Humanist*.